# APPALACHIAN
## REVIEW

**VOL. 52, NOS. 1-2**
**WINTER/SPRING 2024**

**TRADITION. DIVERSITY. CHANGE.**

ESTABLISHED IN 1973
PUBLISHED QUARTERLY
by Berea College
www.appalachianreview.net

©2025 by Berea College. Vol. 52, No. 1-2, Winter/Spring 2024. All rights reserved. No part of this publication may be reproduced without the prior permission of *Appalachian Review*. Periodicals postage paid at Berea, Kentucky, and at additional mailing offices. ISSN# 2692-9244 (Print); ISSN# 2692-9287 (Digital).

Electronic submissions only at www.appalachianreview.net. Distributed through a partnership between the University of North Carolina Press and Duke University Press. Basic subscription price: $32/year for individuals, $64/year for institutions. For subscription requests and inquiries, visit the magazine's website, email subscriptions@dukeupress.edu, or call 888-651-0122 (toll-free in the US and Canada) or 919-688-5134.

# CONTENTS

**COVER PHOTOGRAPH**

*Cherry Blossoms* by Mac

# EDITOR'S NOTE

## JASON KYLE HOWARD

A few months ago, we got a new dog. A rescue, estimated age one-and-a-half to two years. She's had a hard time—one look in her eyes will tell you that. She came from a dog hoarding situation in Pulaski County, Kentucky—Harriette Arnow country, for all the Appalachian scholars out there—and an owner who had dementia. She flinches at sudden movements and noises, and that fear, the history it hints at, breaks my heart. I can't imagine what she's experienced.

Three months after we adopted her, though, she's starting to settle in. We've paid close attention to her body language, tried to decipher what she is communicating, what she needs. I know she is doing the same with us. We're all learning in this new space. Our beagle, Ari, has assumed the role of mentor to her. He's already her best friend. And she's taken to her new name nicely. Alice Eleanor Roosevelt: the names, freighted with history, of two formidable women, cousins and enemies, from an extraordinary family.

Alice is learning to be our reading and writing companion. She takes turns between me and my husband, curling up next to us in our chairs, or on the floor at our feet. But not for too long. She's young and active. She loves to dash up and down the hill in our backyard.

Alice was by my side as I put together this issue, as I ached for the narrator of Jennifer Dickinson's story "Mallwalkers," hoping for her sobriety, happiness and reconciliation; as I remembered the two Appalachian poets, wordsmiths, teachers immortalized in Marianne Worthington's poignant centos; as I soaked in the lyrical prose that propels Emily Warren's essay about her ancestral land in Eastern Kentucky.

So many lessons—on writing, on relationships, on life—can be found in the stories, essays and poems contained in this issue, and particularly in the interview, in which poet-children's book author-young adult novelist-novelist-memoirist-songwriter George Ella Lyon talks with Silas House about the "Olympic patience" it takes to be a writer and the importance of listening.

"[P]art of the joy of revision is you get to listen more," George Ella says, "and you're not in that first draft, falling in love sort of state that can be so intoxicating. I used to say that first drafts are like falling in love and second drafts are like marriage. You know, from then on, you've gotta work on this stuff. It's not just [gasps]. There's life to be worked out, but you learn."

As I write this note and think on George Ella's thoughtful observation, my eyes turn to Alice. She's splayed out on the blue-and-cream rug in my office, asleep and dreaming. I study the tips of her white teeth, barely visible beneath her beard. One of her hind legs is moving as if she might be running in a dream. What's she chasing, I'm not sure. But I hope she has found some measure of security in this house with us and, as time goes on, we will get to know each other better. By listening, by learning, by loving. ■

# 2023 DENNY C. PLATTNER AWARDS

The annual Plattner Awards were established in 1995 by Kenneth and Elissa Plattner to honor their late son and his love of writing. The awards are given to the finest pieces of fiction, creative nonfiction, and poetry that appeared in *Appalachian Review* during the previous year. Winners receive a $200 prize, and both winners and honorable mentions are awarded a handsome piece of handmade ceramics designed and manufactured by Berea College Crafts.

## FICTION
Winner: Jeff Wallace, "Relief, Relief"
Honorable Mention: Mary Carroll Moore, "Downstream"

## CREATIVE NONFICTION
Winner: Lindsey Pharr, "On Being Still and Knowing"
Honorable Mention: Ann Pancake, "Yellow Jackets"

## POETRY
Winner: Josh Nicolaisen, "My Bluebird"
Honorable Mention: Lucas Warren, "Orpah"

# MALLWALKERS

JENNIFER DICKINSON

T he subject of the email stood out like a neon sign. *Call the office to schedule your vaccine appointment.* My heart began to vibrate.

"Hello, this Caroline Pembleton," I said in a rush when Linda picked up. "I need to get the shot."

"Dr. Giardello said you'd be calling. We want to get all our patients in the vulnerable category taken care of as soon as possible. You staying active?"

"Mostly," I said. "I was walking. And then it got so cold, so I stopped. But I'm keeping up with my jumping jacks."

Linda had been the one to show me how to do them right, keeping my hands straight and my legs strong.

"Great. First available appointment is next Tuesday."

"Where do I go?"

"The old Dillard's out on Landers Creek."

My breath caught.

"Do you know where that is?" Linda asked.

Of course I did. The store is where I set fire to my life.

I steadied my breathing. "Is it being offered anywhere else?"

"No, and it won't be for a while. Do you need transportation? I can arrange it."

The world got fuzzy. I grabbed hold of the kitchen chair.

"No, that's okay. I'll go."

"Ten a.m. And Dr. Giardello wants me to say that you may experience flu-like symptoms after you get the shot. Don't be alarmed. Take Advil. Drink fluids."

We hung up and I tapped my heart. Morse Code for: "I love you." Dr. G. taught it to me after the surgery. He said I needed to give my heart positive reinforcement every day. I always thought he might have the hots for me and I only got more suspicious when he demonstrated the Morse code thing. But I did it every day.

■ ■ ■

The day of my appointment I watched an old episode of Anna's show that I'd DVRed. My DVR was a sea of *Loved and Lost*, the soap opera Anna had been starring in for the last twenty years.

"You have to go, Heath!!" she sobbed, flinging herself across the fainting couch.

"Francesca, I'm in love with you." He grabbed my daughter and pulled her in for a kiss. A long one with tongue.

"I'm never leaving you," he whispered.

There were tears in both of their eyes.

Anna sobbed even more. "I'm terrified of dying alone."

I turned off the television. I'd started to tear up, too, even though I knew Francesca would never die. She was the most talented person on the show, her sobs seemed real. They were so real, I believed, because Anna was remembering what happened between us.

Anna never gave many interviews and she'd only mentioned me once, saying we were estranged. When the reporter pressed her for details, Anna said it was an awful story she would take to her grave. That made two of us. The one man I'd told acted like it wasn't a big deal but when we had our only fight, he told me only a broken person would've done what I did. I wanted to say *screw you*, but then I realized he was right. I didn't date anyone else after that.

I opened my desk drawer and pulled out the yellowing letter that I'd started thirty years ago, at the direction of my therapist in rehab: "Apologize to your daughter. Make amends."

I made amends with the manager at my job at the hospital, where I'd regularly snuck drinks in the bathroom. I made amends with my mother, whose car I'd wrecked. But Anna was a different story. I imagined her at her new school in LA telling her friends: "My mother died. I never knew her." She was better off not hearing from me.

My therapist persisted, so I tried. *Dear Anna, I've been thinking about writing you every day, but I was always afraid.* Afraid didn't cover the agony that gripped me imagining Anna trying to forget me. I never finished the letter.

Since my bypass surgery, I tried to write it again, but never finished. Time passed. Covid killed so many. And though my heart grew stronger, my courage got weaker. I didn't know what I could say to make things right with my daughter, to erase the past. But I needed to stay alive if I ever wanted a chance at doing it.

■ ■ ■

At the entrance to the mall, I found a sign stuck to a stake, handwritten: *Vaccines—Follow Arrows*. Bird doo-doo all over the words. Definitely an omen.

There were no cars behind me, so I sat staring into the vast expanse of the shopping complex, disappearing into the past I'd fought for years to forget. There I was thumbing through Beatles records at Turtle's, buying geraniums at Home Depot. And then there was the terrible memory, the one that gave me nightmares for years and years.

This was a bad idea.

A car honked behind me and I drove, swallowing the lump that grew more monumental with each second that passed. What had I done when I first got sober? Deep breaths. Oh yes. And picture a river. Feel the flutter of a bird's wings against my cheek. Hear the gentle gurgle of a bubbling brook. I tried to picture these things and hear these sounds and feel these things but I couldn't.

The news had been reporting the challenges of getting a vaccine and I'd imagined throngs of people waiting outside the door, but there was no one waiting. Somehow this seemed worse than seeing a bunch of people. If I was the only one in there besides a nurse, I'd be thinking about my daughter and I'd probably cry. In front of a stranger. And even if the person was trained to be around sad people, I didn't want to lose it in front of a person I didn't know. The last person I'd cried in front of was the man, Sam, who'd called me a tragic figure.

I was a dammed river. A dead bird. A kitten who'd fallen down a well.

I pushed open the door, my stomach churning. I followed more arrows to a desk where a man wearing an earring took my ID and scrawled my name on a small white card.

"Congratulations, Caroline," he said, handing me the card. "You're getting vaxxed."

I took a seat in an area with some other grey-haired people. Loud music played. Buddy Holly's "That'll Be The Day." A woman sitting beside me tapped her feet in time to the beat.

I stared down at the marble floors, remembering how I'd gotten my first training bra at the store back when it was called May Cohen's. Robert had bought me a diamond pendant here for our first anniversary. A new song came on. "Sugar, Sugar." The woman beside me hummed along.

I looked across the room at the empty space, but then the empty space became dresses. Racks and racks of them. And Anna was hiding playing hide-and-seek with me. I was chasing after her, dodging women, giggling along with my daughter.

*I ran out of the store and to the other side of the mall. I tore off my mask and threw up in a patch of weeds littered with cigarette butts.*

"You are my candy girl," the woman sang quietly beside me. I clasped my chest. *Anna.* She was gone.

"Caroline Pembleton," a woman wearing a nurse's coat said. I stood up.

The nurse led me to an area behind a curtain, back where the jewelry counter would've been. She gestured for me to take a seat on a vinyl chair.

"I'm Amanda. I'll be giving you your shot today, Ms. Pembleton."

She had a sweet Southern accent and it was a tonic to my nerves. I needed to get this over with and get the heck out.

"Hi," I said.

"How are you doing today?" She took a syringe out of a box.

"I'm fine."

"I'll be quick."

She was. She put a Band-Aid on my arm. "You'll need to wait fifteen minutes so we can make sure you don't have a reaction to the shot."

"I can't wait here."

"You really should."

"Thank you."

I started back toward the door. There were more people in the seating area, and Elvis was playing "Love Me Tender." My eyes darted back to where the dresses had been and what I saw stopped me. Anna. Robert. The salesgirl. Anna in Robert's arms. Anna's lips were blue.

I ran out of the store and to the other side of the mall. I tore off my mask and threw up in a patch of weeds littered with cigarette butts.

I threw up until I gagged, until my eyes were pools of water. I sank to the sidewalk.

"Did the shot make you sick?" a voice said.

I looked up to find a man with a thick head of white hair staring down at me, the lower half of his face covered by a mask.

I wiped my mouth, certain there was vomit on it. I didn't want a stranger seeing me like this. I pulled my mask back up and stood. I nearly fell over. The man grabbed hold of my elbow. I yanked my arm away.

"I need to go home," I said.

"You might should rest here a bit longer."

Why was this man talking to me?

I started to leave, but my legs were jelly. I stopped. So did he.

"I'm Marvin. What's your name?"

"Caroline," I whispered.

"Caroline, do you want to hear a joke?"

I didn't.

"This morning I decided to weigh myself and I said, *Hey! I've lost ten pounds*." He paused. "Then I looked down and saw my stomach resting on the sink."

He stared at me.

"Not too funny, I guess," he said.

I started off again and he was on my tail.

"If you came here to shop, I've got bad news."

Another joke. This time I felt the corners of my mouth turn up a little. I was grateful for my mask. I didn't want to give Marvin the wrong idea.

I got back in my car.

Marvin waved as I drove away.

■ ■ ■

I woke up in a sweat. My forehead was burning. Chills wracked my body.

Anna, my baby. Her little button nose, her blue eyes. She cut a tooth earlier than any baby the doctor had ever seen. "That's a sign of intelligence," the nurse whispered, winking at me as I stood next to a mother holding a whining toddler. "I bet you'll have no trouble with her." There were only temper tantrums when we had to go to Robert's mother's and she wanted Anna to pose for pictures in the dresses she'd embroidered for her. "No like!" Anna had wailed and I'd leaned into her ear and said softly, "Me neither."

I threw off the covers and put on my robe. I wanted a drink. Right now. One sip wouldn't mean I'd completely screwed up, right? No one would ever have to know. I paced my kitchen. I had gone so long without it. Could I really do this to myself? Undo all the years when I'd made a better choice. But the taste of it, how it warmed my throat first, then my stomach, how it drowned my thoughts. One taste and I would feel like the universe had righted itself. The walls were so close. My breath was strangling me. I walked out the front door.

I eyed my car. I could drive to the store, but I knew I'd chicken out before I went in. There were trash cans lining the road. Trash night. Thank God. I ran outside and began throwing open lids, my hands reaching inside and searching for liquor—one drop and I could go inside and sleep again. I landed on a bottle and I knew what it was just by the shape of it. Myers's Rum. I unscrewed the cap and inhaled the musky sweetness. My teeth chattered so much, it was like they were playing a song. I brought the bottle to my lips. Headlights flashed. The beams blinded me for a second and I saw what I was about to do.

I dropped the bottle and ran back into the house. I had Roxie on speed-dial, though we hadn't spoken in a couple of years. The last time I'd come close to drinking was when the article came out where Anna said we were estranged.

"Caroline?" she said drowsily.

Tears choked my words.

"Are you okay?"

I couldn't answer.

"Hold on." I heard her mumbling to someone.

"What's going on?" she asked a few seconds later.

I told her about the shot, seeing Anna in the store, how I'd gone searching for booze.

"I want you to take some deep breaths with me now," she said when I finished talking.

"In through the nose, out through the mouth. Three times."

I did it because she told me to. Loudly. My thoughts were still so mixed up, like they'd been put in a blender and turned to high.

"Let's say the prayer," she said. *"God grant me the serenity..."*

I said the words, but I was just going through the motions. My mind was still back outside, holding the bottle. I'd gotten so close.

"You are not your past, remember?"

"Yes," I said.

"Have you been connecting with your HP?"

My Higher Power. Roxie and I had decided I would connect with Him through knitting. There were at least twenty sweaters now, in all different sizes and colors. I didn't have anyone to give them to, and the pile got too big after a while, so I'd stopped.

"Kind of."

*I said the words, but I was just going through the motions. My mind was still back outside, holding the bottle. I'd gotten so close.*

I wiped my eyes. I needed to get a hold of myself.

"You know what comes next."

I did. And I didn't want to do it. Just like I didn't want to knit another useless sweater.

"I need to be of service," I said.

"Yes. Why don't you go to a meeting tomorrow? Set up the chairs? Or bring one of your coffee cakes. You need to get out of your head. Stop thinking about number one."

"Okay."

"I'm proud of you for not drinking again. That is huge."

"Thank you."

"Remember. Take it one day at a time. And call me tomorrow, okay? I want you to check in with me every day for a week."

"Okay."

When I got up in the morning, my fever was gone, but I felt like my body and mind had been through a war. I wrapped myself in an afghan on the sofa. I watched Anna's show.

■ ■ ■

I called Roxie every morning. I told her I'd brought my coffee cake to two meetings and that I'd given spare change to a homeless person and sent money to the Red Cross. I hadn't left my house. She said she was proud of me and to get in touch if I needed any more help. I watched Anna's show. I pressed my forehead against her face.

■ ■ ■

I got an email about my second vaccine appointment.

"Make sure you remember to go," Linda wrote. "Otherwise the vaccination won't work."

What did it matter now? It was as if by searching for a bottle, I'd actually taken a sip. But I hadn't. I was still hanging on.

■ ■ ■

There were more people waiting this time. My pulse was racing and I did my best to not let my eyes wander around the store. The boy with the earring waved me over.

"Can I have your card, ma'am?" he asked.

*Ma'am.* That's what the salesgirl said: "Ma'am, we were looking for you everywhere." Robert had looked at me, his eyes bleary. "No more chances," he'd said.

There was an exit behind the boy, an opening to the rest of the mall.

"I need a minute," I told him.

I found a bench just outside the opening and I sat down.

A river. A stream. A brook. I closed my eyes.

"You're back," a voice said. I opened my eyes and saw the man, Marvin, who'd talked to me in the parking lot before. He wore shorts. It was twenty-five degrees outside.

"You want to take a walk?" he asked.

"It's snowing."

"I come inside the mall to get my steps in. I can't walk outside in this shitfuck weather."

I found myself smiling behind my mask. *Shitfuck*. I'd never heard anyone say that before.

"The mall's closed," I said.

"Not quite. Next to the old Sears there are still a couple of stores open."

If I went home, I might drink.

"Alright," I said.

"Okay, Caroline. Let's get this thing done."

I followed him to the escalators, which were stopped. The air smelled like musty papers and it took me a second to get my bearings and realize we were standing next to the old food court, but there were no tables or chairs. The signs for Sbarro and McDonald's and Panda Express were gone, the metal gate doors shuttered. I imagined I saw Robert and Anna sitting at a table, drinking milkshakes and eating fries. I glanced back at the door, my breathing was tight, it felt like before the heart surgery, like there was an elephant sitting on my lungs.

"The store over there sells clothes for girls who want to look like ladies of the night," Marvin said, pointing to a store where music spilled out, blaring. Mannequins stood outside.

One wore a bright orange miniskirt and a white crop top. Another wore a sequined pink dress.

"Then there's a store that'll make you keys, and a jewelry store. Not much left."

The fluorescent lights flickered. The mall had become a tomb.

"It's strange here," I said. "Kind of creepy."

"I picture it like the Parthenon. A place that used to be magnificent a long time ago."

"You couldn't get pepperoni pizza at the Parthenon," I said. A joke. It slipped out before I could think twice. It probably wasn't funny. But Marvin laughed.

"I used to come here with my family," he said. "A long time ago."

"Me, too."

Our eyes locked.

"I'm not much of a talker," I said.

"Well, I can listen to my podcast," Marvin said.

He put headphones on. We set off.

He walked briskly and so did I. I'd gotten up to two miles before it turned to winter and it felt good to move my legs again. I was never an athlete, but I always liked a lot of activity. Activity kept me from dwelling in the past.

We went in circles, around the perimeter of the mall, past empty stores. Stickers announcing half-price sales peeled off the murky glass windows. The lights were dimmer in certain areas and it felt like a war had taken place, like there should've been shrapnel on the floor instead of dust bunnies.

When Marvin stopped, I could've gone longer. My heart was clattering around my chest, but in a good way. The elephant was gone.

Marvin took off his headphones.

"I'll be here tomorrow," he said.

"Same time?" I asked.

He nodded. "You're coming back?"

"Yes."

His eyes crinkled. He was smiling.

Marvin walked me to my car, and waved again as I pulled away. A part of me wanted to stay with him and I didn't understand why.

That night, I woke up thinking about Anna and her eyes and her nose and my legs hurt like the dickens. I tapped Morse code on my chest. I got up to take some ibuprofen. Then I wandered over to the cabinet.

When I first stopped drinking, I accomplished my weekly act of service by joining a church just so I could contribute to the fellowship time. At first the women badgered me about why I wasn't in service with them, but then they tasted my brownies and never asked about it again.

The best part of baking for the church was that women talked to me while they ate. They opened up about things: one

*Marvin walked me to my car, and waved again as I pulled away. A part of me wanted to stay with him and I didn't understand why.*

had emailed an ex and he'd told her to take a hike, one was furious at her cousin for blowing off their wedding reception. I gave advice: take deep breaths, connect to God any way they could—this came more easily for them than for me since I'd never been a believer. A woman told me, while inhaling my divinity, that she was a lesbian and she was terrified to come out to her family. Her father was the pastor. I hugged her and told her I was sorry and that maybe this wasn't the right church for her. Last I heard she'd moved in with her aunt in Portland.

Maybe Marvin would like some cake. I dug past cans of tomato soup and tuna fish until I found a yellow box cake and one of those containers of chocolate frosting. I bought them a long time ago on sale. I checked the expiration dates. They were just under the wire. A few more weeks and they'd be trash.

I finished the cake and ate a slice at my kitchen table. I remembered baking cakes with my daughter, how she'd loved to lick the bowl. I went to my desk and got a fresh piece of paper and a pen.

*Dear Anna, I am not the same woman I was. I hope you can forgive me.*

I stared at the words until they blurred. They were even stupider than my first attempt. I crumpled up the paper and threw it in the trash.

■ ■ ■

I walked in at another entrance, so I wouldn't have to go through Dillard's. Marvin stood by the escalators, in shorts again. His calves were slender and shapely. I sucked in my breath. An old woman like me had no business thinking about an old man's legs.

"I brought something," I said.

I opened my bag and pulled out a tin-foil wrapped plate.

"How did you know it's my birthday?" he asked.

"It is?"

"No," he said. "Ha-ha."

He pulled off his mask. He had a mustache as white as his hair. His smile made me smile. He took a bite of cake.

"Shit woman, this is great. I was feeling a bit blue this morning, and I'm not talking about my balls."

I burst out laughing. Marvin could surprise me so easily.

"You cheered me up," he said.

I wondered why he needed cheering up, but I didn't feel comfortable enough with him yet to ask.

He finished the cake and sighed. He put his mask back on.

"Now I really gotta get some exercise," he said. "Shall we?"

■ ■ ■

The next day I stopped us walking just as we'd started and pointed to the store with clothes for ladies of the night. Marvin had made me laugh. More than a few times. I wanted to make him laugh. He took off his headphones.

"Let's go in and buy something," I said.

He was quiet. Maybe my plan wouldn't be funny. I kept going, anyway.

"We'll say it's for our friend," I said.

His eyes lit up. Butterflies started a party in my stomach.

"Our granddaughter," he said. "That'll be funnier."

The music was three times as blaring in the store. I wanted to cover my ears. A woman with long dark hair and long purple fingernails slouched on a stool behind the counter.

"Can I help you?" she asked.

"We need something slutty," Marvin said.

The girl didn't hear.

"We need something for our granddaughter!" I shouted, stifling a giggle.

The girl raised an eyebrow.

"Hmmm," she said, and we all studied the sequined tops and studded belts and shiny high heels.

"What kind of stuff does she like?" the girl asked.

"Tight stuff," Marvin said.

"Short stuff," I said.

"Favorite color?" the girl asked.

"Purple," Marvin said at the same time as I said: "Pink."

"I have a pink and purple striped sweater over here," the girl said.

"You have anything tighter?" Marvin asked.

The girl's eyebrow shot up again.

"How old is your granddaughter?"

"Fifteen," I told her.

I heard Marvin laugh. Our eyes met. I didn't want to look away.

"What about this?"

The girl walked over to a rack and grabbed a purple swath of fabric.

"It comes in pink, too. It's really popular."

I touched the material. It was scratchy and there was glitter sewn into the seams.

"What is it?" I asked.

"A bikini top?" Marvin guessed.

"A bandeau top," the girl corrected. "She can wear it with jeans."

Anna didn't dress this tacky even on a show where her role was to have love affairs with all the available men.

Marvin paid $13 for the $12.99 top, and told the girl to keep the extra penny as a tip. She rolled her eyes.

We left the store and Marvin high-fived me.

"That was fun," he said.

"That was," I said.

"You should keep this," Marvin said, handing me the top when we reached our cars. "A memento."

I felt my face get hot, a wildfire on my cheeks.

"I'll be out of town for a few days," he said. "Visiting my horse's ass of a sister in Virginia."

I laughed but I wanted to ask him not to go. We had a routine. I pictured myself at home, thinking about doing my jumping jacks and not doing them, tapping Morse code on my chest. Calling Roxie again. It was a scene I didn't want to live.

"Do you know how to text?" Marvin asked, pulling out his phone.

"I'm younger than you."

"Oh yeah?"

We typed our numbers into each other's phones and got into our cars.

My phone pinged a few hours later.

A text from Marvin: "I like you."

I dropped the phone like it was made of razorblades. I didn't know what to say. But I kept re-reading the text. No one had liked me in a long time. Well, Dr. G., maybe. But he had probably just taken pity on me because of my weak heart.

The next day I didn't do my jumping jacks and I kept thinking about Marvin's text and how I hadn't replied. I needed to run my body down so my mind would have a chance of quieting. *Shitfuck*, I thought and smiled.

■ ■ ■

It was boring without Marvin to sneak looks at, but my muscles had gotten used to moving and woke up quickly. I'd made my last lap when a petite brunette waved to me. I didn't recognize her. She came over.

"You walk with that man, right?" she asked. She seemed nervous, her eyes large above her mask.

I nodded.

"Where is he?"

"Visiting relatives in Virginia. Why?"

Was this woman after Marvin? If she was, I had news for her. He liked me.

"Phew," she said. "He seems so fit, but when a person gets old you never know. I'm glad he has a friend. We've been worried about him."

"Who was worried?"

"The other women that work with me. At the jewelry store." The woman pointed behind her.

"Why?"

"Because of his daughter. He came in once and told us. We were all so shocked."

What was she talking about?

"You know what happened, right?"

I shook my head, a pit growing in my stomach. News I wouldn't like was on its way.

"You remember the shooting here? Like forever ago...the eighties maybe?"

The shooting. I remembered news stories about the mall. Kids killed.

"His little girl died that day," the woman said. "We couldn't understand why he would ever want to come back here. Strange. Anyway, I've been meaning to talk to you two—our lease is up in a few weeks and soon the whole mall will be..."

The woman kept talking, but I'd gotten lost. Poor Marvin. To lose his daughter here. Awful.

I texted Marvin later: "The mall is shutting down soon."

"Ain't that some shit," he texted back and then a minute later: "We better get our walks in. I'm home Tuesday. You want to go Wednesday?"

"Sure," I wrote back.

■ ■ ■

That night I Googled *Landers Creek mall shooting* and two articles popped up. I scanned the first. It happened on December 28, 1982. Three kids and two adults had been killed by a twenty-five-year old named Jim Purdy. Back then shootings in public places were an anomaly so there were no protocols in place to deal with such a tragedy. It took hours to apprehend Purdy as he'd hidden in various stores. The article talked about how the shooting was "unheard of." Nowadays the shooting would be unremarkable.

The second article listed the victims' names. There was only one little girl. Isabel Howard, age seven.

My eyes welled up. What would it have been like if Anna died that day?

It nearly happened.

"Mama is going to run one quick errand out to the car," I'd told Anna when we got into the ladies' lounge. "You stay right here like a good girl. Eat this lollipop and I'll be right back."

She'd looked at me with her large blue eyes and taken the candy.

I'd been sober for thirty days. My sponsor at AA called me a champion. But I wasn't a champion. I spent my nights sneaking a bottle of Stolichnaya out of the cabinet in the

*I ran. The car was just outside the mall doors and the vodka was under the passenger side seat. One swig and I could breathe again without wanting to cry.*

laundry room and staring at the liquid, wishing it was inside of me, rinsing away the memories I had of my past.

I ran. The car was just outside the mall doors and the vodka was under the passenger side seat. One swig and I could breathe again without wanting to cry.

But it was more than one sip. It was a lot of sips. Raindrops pummeled the windshield. I turned the car on and then the radio. A station was playing Carole King's greatest hits. How absolutely perfect. I reclined the seat. I closed my eyes.

I woke with a jump. Anna. I checked the clock. I'd been gone thirty minutes. I ran back into the store. I went to the ladies' lounge but she wasn't there. I tore through the dress department, checking under the racks, calling her name. Nothing.

Customer Service. I ran there. "I've lost my daughter," I told the girl at the counter.

"What does she look like?" she asked. I wanted to shake her.

"Ma'am," a voice said.

I turned around to find another girl staring at me. "Are you Caroline Pembleton?" she asked.

I nodded, my head throbbing.

"Ma'am, we were looking for you everywhere."

Robert appeared behind her. He held Anna in his arms. Her lips were the color of her the sky on the summer days we loved so much. The whites of her eyes were speckled red. I touched her forehead. She smiled weakly.

I started to talk but he held up in his hand. "She choked on the candy you left her with. She almost died."

I'd started crying then, desperate cries. People turned. Robert stared at me coldly.

"I told you. No more chances."

I knew he was remembering all the crimes I'd committed. I'd forgotten Anna at pre-school so often that now another mother brought her home. The stove caught on fire when I forgot I was making her mac and cheese. The kitchen had to be remodeled. Anna wore a scar on her left hand from picking up scissors I'd left her with when she was barely three.

After that day at the mall, Robert hired a lawyer who sent letters to me, threatening ones. One of the letters said: *For Anna's mental health, we need her to move on from you.* I called and called until Robert changed his number. I was drinking again, living out of my car, eventually moving in with my mother who encouraged me to sign away my rights. "You're not a mother," she told me. "You're a failure." I didn't have a fight in me to fight for my daughter. I never saw Anna again.

I wanted to tell Marvin I knew about Isabel and I was so sorry but when I saw him standing outside waving, I didn't know if I'd be able to say anything. I wasn't a brave person. I worked for decades as the bookkeeper at a hospital where I hid away in my office because I never wanted to get close to anyone. The only family I had was the one Anna had created on her soap opera. I knew about all of her marriages, her five children. I cried when she cried.

My walks with Marvin were the best thing that had happened to me since I gave birth to my daughter. I didn't want to risk losing them.

I got out of my car. With each step I took toward Marvin, my stomach buckled with nerves. When I reached him, I noticed his eyes. They seemed warmer than usual.

"You want to hear a joke?" he asked.

I nodded.

"A pirate walks into a bar with a steering wheel coming out of his crotch..." he said.

I laughed when he finished, though I hadn't followed him to the punchline.

We went into the mall. It felt darker than usual. The music was off at the store for the ladies of the night.

"How was seeing your sister?" I asked.

"She's still a horse's ass," he said. He put on his headphones. We started walking. My heart was full of regret, enough shitfuck to go around for a hundred people. I grabbed Marvin's arm. He took off his headphones.

"You all right?" he asked.

"I know about your daughter," I blurted out. "I'm sorry."

Marvin didn't say anything and I was certain I'd messed things up. Thinking about his past was probably the last thing he'd want to do. I started to leave. He touched my arm.

"Wanna get out of here?" he asked.

"Yes."

■ ■ ■

Marvin lived a few miles away, in a one-story brick house at the rear of a cul-de-sac. A large maple tree took up the bulk of the yard. He parked in the carport and I parked behind him.

He stood at the open front door, waiting for me.

"Welcome," he said and gestured for me to go ahead. I entered a living room, which was neat and spare. A sofa and a chair and a coffee table. A trumpet stood up against a stand in the corner.

"Why don't I get us some water?" Marvin asked.

I took a seat on the sofa. There was a framed photo on the coffee table—a much younger Marvin with a red-haired woman standing beside a red-haired little girl. They were on top of a mountain. My mouth went dry. The little girl must've been Isabel. Marvin and his family looked so relaxed. I had pictures like this of me and Anna and Robert, taken before drinking consumed my life.

When Anna turned three, I started having nightmares of being in a dark room while a pair of hands I couldn't see touched me in places the hands weren't supposed to go. I'd wake up crying and I started sneaking to the kitchen and drinking tablespoons of vodka so I'd be able to sleep again. Robert caught me and begged me to tell him what was going on, but I couldn't put into words what I didn't understand. The memories started being all day and I couldn't look at Anna without remembering the abuse, of seeing me as her. I did the only thing I could: I drank.

"It's been a while since I had a woman in here," Marvin said, setting a glass of water down on coffee table in front of me. I removed my mask and took a sip. Marvin watched me. I wondered if he liked what he saw. Marvin removed his mask and took a sip. There was his smile again. He had a kind face, one I felt I could trust.

"What happened to your wife?" I covered my face again.

"Diana died three years ago," he said, covering his. "She battled breast cancer for a long while."

"I'm sorry."

"What about you? Are you married? Were you married?"

"My husband left me when our daughter almost died…"

"What happened?"

The question hung in the air. I didn't know how to answer, where to start. If I told him about the awful day, I'd be conjuring Anna into the room and if I was going to do that to her, I had to tell about other things. Anna wasn't just that day. She was so much more.

"My daughter loved the scarecrow," I said.

Marvin studied me. It had been so long since I'd thought about things like this, happy things, and a warmth enveloped my chest.

"I read her a picture book of *The Wizard of Oz* and she kept pointing to him, saying: *Mama, me love.*" I smiled. "I got her a puppet and she was obsessed with him. Wanted to sleep with him at night."

"What else did she love?"

"Strawberry ice cream. And ladybugs. We used to have so many in our backyard. I remember one day I fell asleep on a blanket and I woke up to her putting a ladybug on my nose."

I could still feel the tickle of the insect's feet. Anna's bright blue eyes staring into mine, inches away. Remembering these things was like opening up a cave inside of me, a cave of light.

"What was your daughter's name?"

"Anna." I took a deep breath. "We haven't talked since she was four. I want to, but I don't know what to say. I don't know how to make things right."

I could hear the faint ticking of a clock. The heat turned on, a blast of warm air above my head.

"My daughter was Isabel," he said. "She wanted to be a famous drummer someday."

"What else did she love?"

"Football. Road trips."

He looked down at his lap. I knew he was lost his past, and I knew about doing this. The past is where I'd stayed lost for the last thirty years.

"You play?" I asked, gesturing toward the trumpet.

"Not very good," he said.

"Will you play for me?"

He walked over to the instrument and picked it up and brought it to his lips. Marvin began to play softly, and then the sound filled up every inch of the room. It took a second for me to realize what he was playing. "Somewhere Over the Rainbow." My hand found my heart. Tap, tap, tap.

"I don't know why I keep this thing," Marvin said, setting the trumpet back against the stand. "I can't play for shit."

"I like it. And I like you." I took down my mask and smiled.

"Oh no," he said. "I think I've given you the wrong impression."

His eyes sparkled. I walked over to him. There was electricity between us, so strong I felt like I might burst out of my skin. I touched his arm. I leaned in and pressed my lips against his.

When we parted, we were breathless.

"You're good for me, woman," he said. "You get me out of my head. I've been stuck there with Isabel these last few months. Missing her something fierce."

I thought of Anna, how lost I'd been. Marvin had gotten me out of my head, too.

"I know what getting stuck is like," I said.

He touched my cheek. A smile spread across his face.

"I've still got some of those little blue pills in the bathroom cabinet."

My heart began to dance a wild dance. "Get them."

He left. I turned over the picture of his family on the coffee table. I took off my shoes, and then my shirt and jeans. I looked down at my bare stomach. My skin was on fire.

He came back. He whistled. "Hot mama."

"Come here," I said, and he did. ■

# ELEGY FOR RON HOUCHIN: A CENTO

Perhaps they are connected to us,
the names of the dead that drift up
as if we're in a dream from this world
waking like a nest in the rain.

The body speaks its own language
like the mumbles of streams, whispers of leaves,
the owl singing its one-syllable lullaby:
another moon will polish the sky.

I do not question what in darkness may come—
it's cancer—because my hands,
as if curled around a mystery,
remember work doesn't end, only changes.

Crows never have the day off,
contemplate the patient hosannas of trees,
the dogs' chorus accompanying the whoop and wheeze
and days of ball bearing skies.

You're a spirit that I see
sitting out on the back steps at night.
We read old letters aloud
in silent syllables, in lines long and green.

It makes me sad that the old cry is gone from words.
I miss you and the beauty
of the world as mostly fire and fright
with edges like teeth.

The river clears its throat for your coming,
the river under blue light.
I keep trying to believe
my soul won't always be orphaned.

## MARIANNE WORTHINGTON

Cento composed with lines from Ron Houchin's complete poetry collections: *Bartley Modern Writers Series* (M.K. Wilkes, 1973), *Death and the River* (Salmon, 1998), *Ron Houchin Greatest Hits, 1976-2002* (Pudding House, 2002), *Moveable Darkness* (Salmon, 2003), *Among Wordless Things* (Wind, 2004), *Birds in the Tops of Winter Trees* (Wind, 2008), *Museum Crows* (Salmon, 2010), *The Quiet Jars* (Salmon, 2013), *The Man Who Saws Us in Half* (LSU, 2013), *Planet of the Best Love Songs* (Salmon, 2017), and *Talking to Shadows* (LSU, 2020).

# [WHO WILL REMEMBER THOSE SONOROUS VOICES]

A Cento for Jeff Daniel Marion

Who will remember those sonorous voices,
that handwritten page, ink blue
so blue I can't believe the years—

where have they gone, those words
like fading names on a weather-washed gravestone?
My heart's hungry for a sprig.

I never knew it would be this hard. I remembered
summer, near dusky dark, lightning,
the long journey home to Tennessee

through pines, a moon full and rising, rising.
O who can understand the heart's yearnings?
so swiftly and silently it all flowed by

as the road unwinds, familiar as lines
searching for something beyond words
leading finally to talk of the dead in the past tense,

vanished like a puff of breath.
Grit your teeth against hard times.
Memory and pain join hands,

a surging hymn, for what has passed.
Let's hear it for the forgotten.
Grab your verses and come trotting, time's

a bitch whose sands have washed our streets,
the sky, and a memory to outlive you
headward into the unnamed and unknown.

Your poems, source of a living
rock from its resting place on the riverbank.
From this heap of jumbled pieces, what can I find?

Water. Witness. Word.

**MARIANNE WORTHINGTON**

Cento composed with lines from Jeff Daniel Marion's final poetry
collection, *Letters to the Dead: A Memoir* (Wind, 2013).

# LOUDER THAN
# BOMBS

## SKYLAR BENSHEIMER

1 983. Morrissey writhes onstage. He twirls a bouquet of gladioli. For those nearest the front, his plastic necklaces are like a metronome, beads clanking against bead and bare chest. The crowd crashes into itself, and the red brick walls of The Haçienda bulge onto Whitford Street. His lyrics hang in a dense cloud over Manchester. *Oh, the alcoholic afternoons,*

*when we sat in your room. They meant more to me than any, than any living thing on Earth.*

This is the Morrissey so many Smiths fans would prefer to remember: the pastels, the impossibly still quiff, the songwriting stuck somewhere between maudlin and tongue-in-cheek. But he's aggressive, too; he'll spit in your eye. I remember the first time I heard them I was seventeen and had just left a bookstore. I flipped through their stack of used CDs: Sisters of Mercy, Small Faces, and then The Smiths. I later learned it was their first album. The cover showed a moody, shirtless Joe Dallesandro with hair covering his face, purple washing out the scene. I knew the name, but I associated them with pretension and never listened. It's not an off-base characterization, though sometimes, pretentious people *do* get it right.

I left and slid the disc into my Monte Carlo's CD player. The plodding drums and dreamy guitar riff spilled through the speakers as "Reel Around the Fountain" began. It's a song that traces its finger down your chest and lingers around the hips. The sex unfolds, unlike so many pop songs of the 80s. It isn't gratuitous or sloppy. *Fifteen minutes with you, well, I wouldn't say no* becomes *shove me on the patio, I'll take it slowly.* There's a violence and a vigor but also a yearning. Really, The Smiths and Morrissey are an amalgamation of the other music I loved—the aggression of Minor Threat and Cro-Mags, the melancholic vulnerability of Elliott Smith—they possessed all of it with the bruising wit of Morrissey's lyrics and Johnny Marr's guitar.

Like so many Smiths fans, and maybe all seventeen-year-olds, I found myself unsure of who I was. I had fits of masculinity but also a desire to embrace the feminine pull I had always felt, so when I moved from the purple album to the orange, *Louder Than Bombs*, with a lovely photo of Shelagh

Delaney on the cover, "Sweet and Tender Hooligan" meant everything to me. Just like the pretty, petty thieves of "First of the Gang to Die," it no longer seemed that I had to choose between masculine or feminine, hard or soft. Morrissey described an appreciation, a love for the in between and the blurry.

I've always been a depressive, too. No other singer has gained quite the reputation for being as miserable as Morrissey is—the "Pope of Mope." When you hear, *If you're so clever, then why are you on your own tonight...I know, 'cause tonight is just like any other night. That's why you're on your own tonight,* a person prone to sadness feels seen, understood. I've had so

*Just like the pretty, petty thieves of "First of the Gang to Die," it no longer seemed that I had to choose between masculine or feminine, hard or soft. Morrissey described an appreciation, a love for the in between and the blurry.*

many nights where the only action I could muster was getting up to turn *The Queen is Dead* from side A to side B. There was nothing I needed more at seventeen than to feel understood and accepted, and Morrissey's music gave that to me.

When I was twenty—perhaps the height of my Smiths-Morrissey adulation—I saw him play at the Riviera Theater in Chicago. I bought my ninety-dollar, non-refundable ticket a few weeks before he made remarks during an interview in defense of Kevin Spacey, who had recently been accused of sexually assaulting minors. My friend and I decided that the money was already spent and gone, so there wasn't any harm in going to Chicago anyway. The crowd was densely packed, and we wound tighter and tighter as showtime approached. He opened with a cover of "You'll Be Gone" by Elvis before addressing the comments about halfway through the show: "If you do not hear the words come from my mouth, I did not say them." I had hope, for a moment, that the man whose songs so often felt addressed to me wasn't what the media and so many fans were calling him, but the interview's audio was released a few weeks later, and he had said everything the print interview quoted.

We no longer have the knitwear, bookish Morrissey of the 80s, nor the denim-clad, solo Morrissey of the 90s. We're left with a bigoted provocateur, a denigrator of immigrants, a defender of rapists. He's a man who laments the supposed absence of English accents in London, alleging an erasure of English identity by the hands of people who do not look like him. It seems a far cry from the "Irish Blood" he sings about with pride. More recently, he gave his support to the anti-Islamic For Britain Movement. Unless you're in agreement, there is no argument for defending him; that is certain, but how should we treat the extraordinary catalogue he has built, and how do fans navigate our dedication to and love of his music?

In the modern "cancel culture," unlike the old one that derailed the careers of artists like Sinead O'Connor and The Chicks, should we no longer see Morrissey live, buy his albums? Probably not. I have little desire to do so. The rebellion of The Smiths and Morrissey was, in part, their propensities to attack power. Think "Margaret on the Guillotine," or any number of songs in which they've lambasted the Royal Family, but there's no rebellion in punching down, in attacking the most vulnerable in our society. There is only cruelty. But Morrissey's music isn't cruel. It's been an escape from the cruelty of being alive, existing as I am.

When the needle drops on "Rubber Ring," and I hear, *When you're dancing and laughing and finally living, hear my voice in your head, and think of me kindly*, I do. I think only of what his music has given me since I first heard him. I agree with Nick Cave. There's a sense of ownership that comes with loving a piece of art; we can feel that it is ours, that it means something singularly unique to us, which creates a divide between art and its creator. I loathe Morrissey, but I cannot give up what his music means to me. ■

# MOON MUSIC

I see you over there,
Trying to hold up your
Little section of the world,
I'm over here, trying to hold
Up mine. Hell, I'd hold up the
Whole dad-blamed thing if I
Could figure out how. In the
Meantime, play me some
Music, some old time
Music, some new wave
Music, some cow punk,
Post-funk, space junk
Music, bang it on a
Trash can with a
Big ol' spoon.
Send your
Song up
In the light
Of the moon,
It doesn't really
Matter if it goes
Nowhere. The only
Thing we ever had to
Do was try, so steady
Your hand and open
Your eyes, sing it
Like a bird in a
Colorado sky.
Hold on tight
To your little
Old tune. Listen

For the harmony.
Help is coming soon.

**JOHN P. LACKEY**

# GEORGE ELLA LYON

George Ella Lyon is a treasure of American literature. Born in Harlan County, Kentucky, she served as Kentucky Poet Laureate in 2015 through 2017. She is the award-winning author of many acclaimed poetry collections, picture books, novels for young adults and adults, a memoir, and plays, and she was one of the earliest contributors to this magazine. Lyon has received numerous awards for her work, and her iconic poem "Where I'm From" has been used as a model for writers in classrooms around the globe.

Lyon recently spoke with current Kentucky Poet Laureate Silas House for his podcast *Writing Lessons*, which focuses on a different topic of creative writing in each episode. House says, "On a personal note, I must tell you that George Ella was also one of the earliest established writers to encourage me as a writer myself, and for that, I am forever grateful. Many other writers will tell you that she is one of the people who first influenced and inspired them."

Lyon and House's conversation centered on writing for children and "the deliciousness of words," and has been lightly edited for length and clarity.

■ ■ ■

**SILAS HOUSE: George Ella, I think of you primarily as a poet, but you've written so much for children, so when I thought about doing a show about picture books, I thought, *I'm going to go straight to the expert.* Everybody seems to think they can write a book for children. They think, for some reason, that's the easiest kind of writing. I would argue that it's one of the more difficult kinds of writing. What do you say to that?**

GEORGE ELLA LYON: Well, I usually say, at the beginning of a picture book workshop or a writing for children workshop, that you gotta get assumptions out of the way. One of them is that it's easy. Another one is that it won't require much of you emotionally—you can keep your distance—which kills any writing, of course. And the other one is: you'll make a lot of money. So, if you can get over that, we can go on.

**George Ella Lyon**
*Photo: Ann W. Olson*

I think when people think it's easy, they think [about] the number of words and not realizing that it's harder to be brief, for one thing. And those words have to do so much. I don't think they have a real respect for children. Paula Fox, a writer for children, said, "Children are not a race apart but ourselves when new." And it's that newness, that wonder that they bring that's so...it gives us life. It takes us back to what's essential. And they ask the real questions that we sometimes just pretend we have answers for, or we don't have answers, so we just go on and do what we're doing. You know, the children just get at the heart of things, and so they require your full heart and all the artistry you can bring to it.

**SH: Right, you can't fool them.**

GEL: No. And you better not preach to them or think you're going to set them straight. 'Cause that's deadly. Also, just because you make up stories for your grandchildren doesn't mean that they're going to work for books.

**SH: I think a lot of people think that writing is easy because telling stories is part of our everyday life. But writing is very different than just telling a story, and it requires a craft being really honed and studied with years and years of work.**

GEL: Yeah, and you have to have Olympic patience.

**SH: For sure.**

GEL: And you have to be stubborn, you know, because of the rejection you're gonna go through, and because a lot of projects just don't work out.

Then you come to find out that it isn't a picture book after all. It might be an essay, or something else, but it's not a picture book. And, when you do the dummy, which is the mockup of where the pages turn, many times that's when you realize it's not a picture book. The page turns don't do a thing for it. Maybe it's a poem, but it's not a picture book. So you just have to read a lot. I mean, people will tell me they wanna write for children and I ask *what books do you read?* And they don't. Or they say, *Where the Wild Things Are*, which is a great book, but—

**SH: It's not the only book.**

**GEL**: It's not the only book! You need to read widely and wildly and study.

**SH: What are the most important elements of writing a book for children, whether that be picture book, middle grade novel, young adult novel, whatever?**

**GEL**: I think it's the voice. It might be the voice of a character, but it might not. But it's the voice that comes in at the level of the child's world. And I feel like I have sort of an inner four- or five-year-old, and an inner thirteen- or fourteen-year-old. And, you know, I can call on that. Not that the characters are me, I don't mean that. I listen. I listen to children, all the time. I mean, I have written down things from school visits, I've written down things from my own kids. But, yeah, I would say it's the voice. It's the voice with any piece of writing. That's where you struggle, and struggle, and struggle, and then suddenly, if it's gonna be there, it's there. And then you may have tons of writing yet to do, but you have the traction and the momentum because that voice is going to lead you where you need to go, and where it wants to go. So you have to trust that—you can't force it.

SH: Yeah, I would say voice is the key to all writing. Robert Morgan was an early teacher of mine, a great writer, a great person, and he told me once that it's not so much about the story you're telling as it's about how you're telling the story. And that has always stuck with me, and it's such a simple thing that really shapes the way that you think about a piece of writing, once you repeat that to yourself.

GEL: Right, right. It's a gift when you get there, but you have to go [down that] road.

SH: Exactly. Right, it's like those—they sound really simple when they're said aloud, but it's really complex figuring out how to do it. It's almost like it's easier said than done.

GEL: I always feel, with any piece of writing, the moment that I'm waiting for is when it has something I couldn't give it.

SH: That's where the magic is.

GEL: That's where the magic is. And that's where the voice is—it's like all you can do for your garden, but you can't make beans.

SH: Yeah, I tell my students all the time that when it becomes organic is when you know you're on the right path—when things just start popping up. So I love that you used the garden, because that's exactly what it's like. Let's talk about picture books specifically. What are the key elements of a picture book?

**GEL**: As I was saying, the emotion, the voice, the deliciousness of the words and the way they harmonize, because children are enchanted by that. It's a big step to reading when children start saying the words of the book and turning the pages— because they've gotten that story shape into themselves—and it's partly because the words have so many sound connections and rhythm connections that they're easy to internalize. So the sound, the rhythm, the emotional trajectory.

Most picture books are thirty-two to forty or forty-eight pages long, and so I compare it to tapdancing in the telephone booth...You don't have much space, you don't have much time, so you have to be as distilled as you can, and you have to make the pages turn, so there's a whole lot to choreograph. My editor I used to work with used to say that it can be like a little play. And, if you think about it that way, how it goes along a flow of pages, where the height of it is, where the turn is, you can sometimes strengthen that by changing what's on what page. And, for me, the dummy's really helpful for that because it's just the same number of pages. If it's thirty-two, you take eight pages, fold them and staple them, and you've got thirty-two pages, and I use Post-it notes for the words, and that way, if it's on the wrong page, I can move it easily. It makes me more flexible, and that's helpful in the process. Plus, if I erase a lot, it makes me think of when I was little and I'd erase through the page, and then I'd cry and all that, so I don't want to do that. But I do read it aloud and turn the pages. I mean, I read everything aloud.

**SH: Me too.**

**GEL**: [By doing that] I can tell when I'm faking it. I can tell when the energy drops.

**SH:** One thing that you said made me think about how psychological the act of writing must be. You must think about things that maybe the reader isn't thinking about when they're reading it, but something registers somewhere in their brain. For instance, the way we use white space, or where to turn the page, and things like that, are really important.

**GEL:** Right, right. And it's also—sound and rhythm and voice are in your body, so you're not just responding with your brain. And I have taken videos of my grandchildren as they're coming along in their relationship with books, and Julian, who's almost a year old—his mom was reading him *Goodnight Moon*, and he kisses the page now.

**SH:** That'll melt your heart.

**GEL:** Yeah. This is how the magic happens, you know. The reaction to books, the trying to get into books. I heard about a little boy, who, his mom found him in the morning—he was a toddler—he had taken off his PJs, he had taken off his diaper, had opened *Goodnight Moon* and he was standing on it as if he could get in there. So, you know, the depth of the reality, the depth of attention, that a child brings to the picture book—it has to be worthy. You're in relationship with this reader.

**SH:** This is important stuff.

**GEL:** It's really important.

**SH:** You mentioned having an inner child, an inner teenager, et cetera, so maybe that's part of the answer to this—but I'm just wondering, when you're writing novels for young readers, whether it's young adult or middle grade, how do you strike the balance of not condescending to them, but also not writing in a way that is too adult, or that goes over their head?

GEL: Again, I think it's the voice, and the depth of the character. I mean, they are intensely *becoming*. From day one, from the womb, they are intensely becoming, and they are questioning...where they're envisioning what could be, because they're not separate yet from the child world or the parental world. It's the difference between being inside or being outside. I mean, you have to be outside to condescend, right—unless there's some psychological condition I don't know about. But you have to be *in*. And if you're really in there, the character is gonna carry who the reader will be. Not that I think middle grade and young adult books are just for readers those ages. Some of them are for—the best of them are for everybody. The picture books as well...

SH: What are some picture books that would be good for aspiring picture book writers to look at?

GEL: Two of my favorites are—and they're very different—one is called *All the World*. It rhymes. It's a poem. And of course they can be poems and not rhyme, but this one does rhyme. It goes through the day so incredibly with this one family, but they're part of a whole community on this little island. And it goes from the beach in the morning, and it takes you through the farmers market, and playing at a tree, and getting caught in this huge rain storm, and going in a restaurant, a diner. But all the people—it accumulates with the people they see at the farmer's market, and one stop to the next. At the end, it's evening, and they're all gathered in this house on the point of the island. They're playing music, and they're all ages and they're all genders and colors. It's just this celebration of community and the wonders of the world. So, that's one, especially because of the illustrations. You can see how the poem, the text, is opened up in such an extraordinary way by those illustrations.

And then there's a book by Patrick McDonnell, and he is both the illustrator and the writer, and it's called *Me, Jane*, and it's about Jane Goodall as a little girl. There's no parents in it, there's no siblings, there's no where she was born, it's just about her and her relationship to the natural world. It's so spare, and the page turn at the very end took my breath away. I'm not gonna tell you what it is, but…[the book] even has a double-spread, which is from her childhood notebook.

**SH: You have mentioned the phrase *the page turn* several times. Would you say that's sort of akin to enjambment in poetry, [where] enjambment can be like the end of the line keeps going, so it leads your eye on? [Of course] that's one thing that enjambment does, but another thing…is that it can change the meaning—you think the line means one thing, then, when you keep reading, it means something else. Is the page turner similar to enjambment, do you think?**

GEL: It can work that way. It can also—you can be very surprised when you turn the page. It can be a quiet shift. It can be something really dramatic that changes. You can come to a full stop too, sometimes, at the end. But what you can't do is start over. The narrative has to keep going. We don't have time. You may get, sometimes, a wordless spread in the middle of a picture book. And that's just right for the book.

And sometimes the illustrator decides that; the writer doesn't decide that. But the page turns can speed it up, they can slow it down, and so can [a] line, in the way a line is moving in a poem. So you can just study the way that's done in different picture books.

And I wanted to say that there are different picture books for much older kids, too. There's a book called *The Little Ships*, I'd say for fourth- and fifth-graders, by Louise Borden, and it's about the evacuation of Dunkirk. She tells it from the point of view of a child who she imagines went over with her dad. And researching that—if you think you don't have to go through any trouble to write a picture book, she found a man who had been one of the soldiers. She wrote to him. She went to England and interviewed him. She crossed the Channel in one of the little boats with him on the anniversary. And had she gotten paid for this? No! No, she was out on a limb.

**SH: You do what you have to do for the book.**

**GEL:** You do. You follow it. And it's extraordinary.

**SH: Just for the benefit of anyone who's thinking about writing picture books and trying to learn more—it's important for us to point out that, most of the time, the writer does not get to pick the illustrator. Can you talk a little bit about that?**

**GEL:** People think you get to tell the illustrator what to do. Well, nobody told you what to do, and it's not your business. Your business is the words on the page, and it doesn't matter what your grandmother looked like...the illustrator has his or her vision. You have to let go.

SH: Yeah, it's a collaboration.

GEL: It is a collaboration, but very odd, because you may have never met and you may never meet, and it's the editor who communicates with both of you. The editor is the spine of the book, in that sense.

SH: You used a phrase earlier that I just loved, "the deliciousness of the words." When I think about your writing, one thing I think about is your fantastical way of using language—the unexpected, the sensory, the interesting. I just think you think about language in a very specific way. And when I think about my favorite writers, I think that a lot of the time, I could maybe read the writing and know who they were because of their certain style and the way they approach language. How do you foster that? How do you make that work better, so that it becomes organic for you as a writer?

GEL: You ask beautiful questions. I'm so glad you said that about the senses, because I should have said that in talking about picture books, that the sensory is so important. I mean, that's what brings something alive, and children are alive to their toes. Things haven't been compartmentalized. My son was sitting on the floor when he was three, and he stood up and fell down, and he didn't know what happened. I said, *Oh, your foot's asleep.* And he said, *No, I got stars in my shoe.*

SH: And that's exactly how it feels.

GEL: And that's almost better! So he didn't need my old handed-down saying, he had his own. And so, again, that refreshment. That wonder. I grew up with good talkers and story-tellers, and I had [the] King James [Bible] and the hymns, and I was read to. And, especially because my daddy read poetry to me, I just thought—well, that's it. That's it.

Something in my own soul responded to the intensity of the language, the melodies, the drama. These weren't poems for kids, and so he once said to me, *I think you must feel about words the way I do about numbers*. And I felt so seen. I mean, I was grown then—or what passes for grown. But I think metaphorically. I just do, and I think I came with that. But when I was revising *Borrowed Children*, the first novel I did for kids—it would be a middle grade—the last thing I had to do was go through with a metaphor rake and take some of them out, because it can get to be too much. And sometimes, like any technique of writing or any aspect of writing, it can become reflexive. Then it's gotta go, because it's subtracting from the work of the work.

**SH: Yeah, I think one of the best writing lessons we can give aspiring writers is to encourage them to revise more. More and more, I talk to people who seem to think you just sit down and it all pours out of you, and you print it out and send it out and it gets published. And, as a young writer, I think that revision was probably ten percent of my process and now it's probably ninety percent of my process.**

GEL: Yeah, people do not want to hear that. They just don't have any idea.

**SH: But I think once you see how it makes your writing bloom you can come to love it, right?**

GEL: Oh, yeah. There's this wonderful book called *Art and Fear: The Perils and Joys of Artmaking*, and they say that— they're photographers—but that creating happens between you and the thing you're creating. Between creator and the thing. And you have to let it speak back to you. So part of the joy of revision is you get to listen more, and you're not in that first draft, falling in love sort of state that can be so intoxicating. I used to say that first drafts are like falling in love and second drafts are like marriage. You know, from then on, you've gotta work on this stuff. It's not just [gasps]. There's life to be worked out, but you learn.

**SH: What's the best writing lesson you've ever learned that you can articulate in just a couple of minutes?**

GEL: I was doing a workshop with fifth-graders in Boyd County, [Kentucky], and I was doing this "Where I'm From" exercise, which is a poem [of mine] that's basically a list of experiences where you're from. And this boy said, "I'm from baseball."

So I said, "Do you play, or do you just watch?"

He said, "Oh, I play."

And I said, "What position?"

He said, "I'm a catcher."

And I said, "Oh, God, I don't think I could stand that mask over my face."

He said, "Oh, I even like it when sweat gets in my eyes."

I said, "Okay, put that in."

The line he came up with is, "I'm from the sweat behind the catcher's mask."

**SH: Oh, that's great.**

**GEL**: And I said, "Wow."

He said, "Oh, I get it, you don't want me to tell you about it—you want me to put you there."

I said, "Yeah, I knew I came here to learn something."

But that's it, you know. That's the miracle, when it happens. That's why we read, too, isn't it? I mean, we read for information, obviously, and we read to learn to think better, but we want to be there. We want to have this other experience; we want our lives to be wider and deeper. So, just put us there. Put us there. ■

# PARADISO

A long time ago Rohan told me
that inside the cabin perched
at the confluence of five hills
next to a crumbling cinderblock
below the floorboards, a hole
leads to an underground passageway
that culminates in a grotto
in which a hot springs
dribbles to perpetuity
since before the dinosaurs.
It's not as easy as I'd anticipated
to arrive at another dimension
that has nothing to do with this one
or to ensure the new diagram of invisible
flames makes it to the right hands.
Where does one go when silence
itself seeps in a sun-fluttered waterspout
and we have no choice except to live
each day in order, one after the other,
even though a single moment can last
longer than anyone can imagine?
If the language of the universe
is god plus a little foreshadowing,
nightly an insurmountable distance
conspires between sentences—
darkness within darkness.
Why should it matter if unfiltered ponds
clamor about the unguided womb?
There's still no word for when
the song in your heart
is the same as the one on the neighborhood

radio. Dante wondered whether or not
Plato was right about the soul returning
to the star where it was born.
All of our words say otherwise.

**ADAM EDELMAN**

# PHOTO ESSAY

You could fit almost anything there:
gray and aimless clouds, early morning
reduced to a close dimness, sealed off
by brief wind. Yet there was hardly room
for the frosted glass vase and the ledger
on the alcove, less and less space
for shade and the glistening sense of shade
as April comes, or June, to a touchable fragrance—
a fertile, unbroken color that is also a pause,
a lifting away of the surface of a pause.

At the bank of the brook, a gesture.
A single emptiness captured as a fragment
of sky. We had wanted to take it with us,
to fold it up and slip it into a wallet
or spread it against the background of a photo
we hadn't seen in years. You can almost see
what the weather's up to in the gaps
between the girders. You can almost hear
the leaf land in a place a leaf has never landed.
The threadbare sky becomes a sound
that looms over the hidden creek
sparkling like a nest with silence.

**ADAM EDELMAN**

# RENDITIONS OF A BARRIER

Viburnum surrounds the observatory.
It only rains in the past. All we see, we see through.
These are nameless shapes; do what you will with them.
There in forsythia, there in a tangle's placeholder—
I didn't think they could get this realized, but they did.
That isn't a pond. Those aren't steeples.

I'm always open to further discussion if you are,
I tell the fence post. According to my research,
all essences are equal expressions of the universal
essence, or something like that.
To put it another way, we are like two pines
on opposite sides of a gorge. I was never
in control. The alley smells of gasoline after dark
as we search for the fence post's voice.

Pay special attention to verges in the brake.
Be sure to keep the carriage covered
when fording a river, for the weight of it is hollow
and full of the noise of nervousness.
It's tough to craft a method for summoning disruption
because it's so simple, like how to draw a circle
big enough to fit in everything: you must begin
by tracing it, then take a step away.

**ADAM EDELMAN**

# BIOPIC

Upon immediate arrival you take note of the post office,
the library, the school. Some of the shops are open, some closed.
I meet you in a corner café, the one with the awning blown out
and a shy cashier, to discuss the movie script we're working on
about the house in the center of town, the huge turreted Victorian,
which displays a different map of the town in each of its rooms.
The film, as you know, is based on a conversation we had
with a local conductor. You remember thinking his face
was like paper with an erased message on it.
"Bells are bells," he had said,
as if something was about to be born. A wish
drew near. You were wearing my favorite jacket of yours,
the one with the silver lining, and couldn't one usually
smooth things over, resolving most differences
at the last possible moment? Flawless,
uncreated beings involve themselves in our cinematic
experiment. We can tell because they tap with exceedingly
soft mallets upon crystalline ears.

**ADAM EDELMAN**

# BLUE DESTINATION

Sure enough, the flowerpot was there
under the window. Something about the flowerpot
suggested a window was nearby,
but it would have to be a plain window
without curtains or additional grandness
other than itself. It would have to be half open,
half closed, the way you were in Los Angeles
below the atrium lit up green
when you couldn't say what love was
but could see plainly what it did to us.
You said the love crisis was unmasked
like a flowerpot, but only to make the riddle
more stretchable, to name the problem
of the hour 'intermittent breeze'
so that these details would appear more relatable
as they were years earlier when we had read less
but could hear more, and the man your sister
was with still saw in the mirror, a kind
of window, someone nearly like himself.
And something in me, a blue destination
in me, wanted to reach out
from the other side of the mirror/window
and tell him no, it is not you,
it's the flowerpot.

### ADAM EDELMAN

# NOCTURNAL WAX

We write plays in our heads based off architectures
of dust in the windowsills, the viewfinder
muddled with basins before and after moonrise
in a blanket of ghost thorns. In a diminishment
of the verge twilight scrawls on,
it wasn't the ripple that entranced us, but overtures
to the russet glen to divulge its anonymous source.
The deer stood still as figurines in a cathedral
as the hunter entered with no bow. A pair
of sunglasses surrounded by minnows.
We wanted not even song, but something
unsure of whether or not to sing, flight
ticket stubs stained with pollen. When I wrote
to you that summer I was eager to convey,
however paltry and unrefined my words
would stand in comparison, some of
the worthiness of simple pleasures like
a corner all of one's own, the details
of a gnat's antenna one observed
there briefly alighting from the small
part of the wall where cheap paint
chipped away, or the scale model of
your own face you imagine looking down
on your house from a mile up.
A magnitude burgeoned, but it died
down a bit to an immaculate scribble.
As when light is evenly diffused
throughout a space, it's the sediment
that germinates in our imagining,
the edits descending a long way
past rural spots in nature. The cornea

inviting nutritious angles, we shovel
driftwood with enhanced, undetectable sprays,
and nocturnal wax is still in print.

**ADAM EDELMAN**

# FINAL FANTASY

I follow the nine gravel paths
from the shuttered motel
to the amphitheater
where the stage is empty and unlit
except for a yellow orange ping pong
ball that I left there previously
to remind myself to separate
the generation of materials
from their arrangement.
You place driftwood
in my mug, say you hear
singing angles in sheet cake
cloud, mountain-cut.
No more harvest festivals
to postpone, gateways
to the netherworld opened.
As I gather the firewood,
a sun without a sky
becomes quite apparent.
A sore throat
takes me out of the diagram.
Sketching a man made of sticks—
I make eye contact with a nervous
rabbit and try to picture
the noteless tune bubbling up
from a higher psychic stratum
before or after belief.
After this we'll have lunch on the park
bench where I met K
and it will seem like coincidence
that both of us strongly considered

leaving a hand mirror there
instead of the ping pong ball.

**ADAM EDELMAN**

# NEST EGG

KAY McSPADDEN

The bus rocked toward the precipice and Charlie's stomach sailed out over the blue mountains and bluer valleys of western North Carolina. Another curve in the road brought his stomach back with a thud. He turned away from the window and looked for something stationary inside the bus to focus on. The passengers across the aisle were no good; their profiles in front of the opposite windows weren't large enough to hide the rocky cliff face that was, in its own way, as alarming as the drop-off view of the valley from his side of the bus.

He'd never gotten seasick on any of the ships he'd served on in the war, and now here he was, struggling not to vomit in a Greyhound. If he were driving a car, the view and the road and the lurching would not be problems. The bus was the problem. The not being in control was the problem. If he had a car—*when* he had a car—he would glide around these hairpin turns with his sea legs intact.

He closed his eyes and thought about the car dealership in downtown Asheville. He'd heard that cars were in short supply. As soon as he stopped at his grandmother's and collected his nest egg, he'd see what was available. A Plymouth or Ford sedan, maybe, though a new 1946 Lincoln Continental better fit what he imagined for himself. Something sleek and stylish to park in front of Eloise's house, not a truck like some local farm boy. A truck wouldn't be worth the money. Even a used Nash would be better than that.

He'd pay cash, peeling the bills from a rubber-banded roll like a movie mobster. He cupped his hand out in front of him, weighing the heft of the invisible money.

"Are you alright?"

Charlie opened his eyes and looked back over his shoulder. The woman behind him was leaning forward, her gloved hand gripping the back of his seat.

"You look a little, you know, *poorly*."

"I don't like riding the bus." Charlie turned to better see the woman but she rose and sat down beside him.

"There," she said. "If you're carsick, you don't want to twist your head around too much. It's not good for you." She opened her flat cloth purse and pulled out a pack of cinnamon-flavored gum. "Chew this. It'll settle your stomach."

"We chewed this all the time aboard ship. Thanks."

"I noticed your uniform. Navy, huh?"

There it was, that note of doubt, or confusion, that he'd heard before when he talked about the war. He knew he looked younger than he was, and he was younger than he should have been.

"Three years, two months, six days."

"You musta joined as a baby."

"The Navy'll take anybody." Charlie laughed as if he were letting her in on a secret. He had, in fact, lied when he enlisted at fifteen. He spent his seventeenth birthday—the day he could have legally signed up—at general quarters on a destroyer rolling depth charges into the Atlantic.

The gum was helping. Charlie peered at the woman's face. Her eyes were light green, like a cat's, and her bobbed hair was dyed the color of straw. He had no idea how old she was—how old any woman was—but he decided she was pretty despite looking tired.

"So what you gonna do now?" she said. "Gonna re-enlist?"

"Not sure," Charlie said. It was true that he hadn't planned very far into the future. Before he could make any plans, he had to retrieve his nest egg first. He'd kept five dollars from his pay for spending money and had the rest—almost fifty dollars each month—sent to his grandmother for safe keeping throughout his deployment. Once he picked up his money and bought a car, he could decide what to do. What he wouldn't do was re-enlist. About that he was sure. He'd been in a stupid rush to join up, propelled by a stew of patriotic fever and boredom. Now he was going to take his time to figure things out.

The woman sighed audibly. "I don't know what I'm gonna do either. I'm waitressing at McCrory's but what I really want is a job at the rayon factory in Enka. Pay's not bad. If you need a place to live, the company has rooms for rent. They even run a train for workers who live in Canton. Ten cents round trip."

Charlie pursed his lips and shrugged. He'd choose a job at McCrory's lunch counter any day over slaving in a textile mill. He'd been inside a cotton mill once. Between the heat and the dust and the cotton lint suspended in the air, he'd struggled to breathe. No, sir. Even working mess duty in the galley of a pitching destroyer was preferable to breaking his back as a spinner in a mill.

"Good luck with that," Charlie said. He met her gaze, grinned, and hitched his voice into a tease. "Your husband don't mind you working?"

The woman's face flushed. "I ain't married. I live with my Ma and my sister. What about you?"

"I'm footloose and fancy free. That's the saying, right? I'm on the prowl."

The woman said nothing. An awkwardness settled around them and he leaned back into the seat. That's what he got for trying to act like he knew what he was doing, worldly and suave and flirty. That's what he got for imitating the older sailors sweet-talking barmaids in port city dives.

"Actually, I'm going to see my grandmother," he said.

The blonde woman looked away.

He tried to remember how old he was when went to live with his grandmother after his mother died, or when he'd last seen his father. Every two or three months his grandmother had awakened him in the middle of the night to help her pack and leave before the rent collector showed up. He lost track of how many houses and apartments they'd fled, how many schools he'd enrolled in, just to start over someplace else soon afterward.

A year before he enlisted in the Navy, he stopped going to school at all and moved to the YMCA near the Biltmore Hotel in downtown Asheville where he found a job as a restaurant bus boy. It was quieter than his grandmother's house, and more predictable. Later he thought that life at sea wasn't that much harder than the life he cobbled together for himself as a teenager, living among strangers and working long hours in a kitchen.

The worst of the hairpins straightened out after the bus passed the small mountain town of Saluda and Charlie's mood lifted as his stomach settled. He studied the blonde woman's profile as she gazed out the window. From this angle she looked younger and less worn down.

"Hey," he said, "they still have those Saturday night dances at The Gloria?"

The Gloria wasn't the only theater in Asheville, but it was the most elegant. The circular ceiling was painted like

*Later he thought that life at sea wasn't that much harder than the life he cobbled together for himself as a teenager...*

twilight—swathes of orange and pink around the rim fading to blue and violet overhead. Pinpricks of light mimicked stars when the house lights dimmed. Like most movie theaters, the screen was mounted on a stage large enough to host performers such as traveling musicians, magic acts, and stumping politicians. On weekends a band played in the orchestra pit while couples paid twenty-five cents to dance on the stage for two hours.

The blonde woman turned to him and nodded. "I think so. I've never been."

"No one's ever taken you dancing?"

"You offering?" A smile tipped up the edges of her mouth.

Charlie's stomach twitched. "I might be."

Of course he wasn't. He had the business of his nest egg to take care of. He couldn't do anything until he had his money and a car. Then there was Eloise. Once he had his car he'd drive to her house and ask her if she wanted to go to the Saturday night dance at The Gloria, and if not, then why the hell not. And while he was at it, he'd ask why her letters to him had been so few.

They'd met at the soda fountain at the Biltmore Hotel, Eloise perched on a red leather counter stool when he passed in front of her carrying a crate of clean glasses from the kitchen. She hailed him for a refill, her voice startling him with its imperiousness. Such a petite person—not much larger than a child—and such a loud, knowing voice. *Waiter, I'm dying for more tea.*

She wore a felt cloche hat—though he didn't know what to call it—and a pink wool coat trimmed in satin. From where he stood, dumbfounded, stupidly holding the crate of glasses, he thought she looked like a storybook princess.

"Well?" she asked, and Charlie looked around for the real waitress serving the counter. She was at the far end chatting with a customer.

"I, uh," Charlie said. "Tea?"

Eloise tilted her head and gave him a look that summed him up so well that he was struck dumb by it.

"Are you being a jokester?" she asked. "Or are you just simple?"

Charlie's face flushed and he hurried to set down the crate and find the pitcher of tea. He pivoted so swiftly that the tea sloshed over his hand and splashed on the painted concrete floor.

He was a teenager, a spray of acne sprouting across his cheeks and nose, a tall, skinny, might-as-well-be-orphaned virgin. She was three years older, a high school graduate, with a father so protective that lunch unchaperoned at the Biltmore Hotel soda fountain was a rare liberty. The puddle of tea on the floor loosened something in them both and they laughed at the same time.

From then on they made a point of meeting on Wednesdays when Eloise came into town. They never did much more than chat, Eloise primly eating open-faced roast beef sandwiches, Charlie helping himself to a free cup of coffee. Sometimes they strolled down the sidewalk as far as the bus station or uptown to the town square. The rest of the week Eloise helped her mother with the house and the younger children. She told Charlie that she wanted to go to secretarial school but her parents were opposed to the idea. Her father owned the local sawmill, which was profitable even when most men were desperate for work. To Charlie, her father's relative wealth might as well have been a dragon's hoard, and Eloise a captive, as if she really were a princess in a fairy tale.

Now, however—three years, two months, and six days after he left to go to war—Charlie came back ready to slay whatever dragons were in his way.

But first, the nest egg.

On the bus, the woman with her green cat eyes stared at him, her brow wrinkling as she made some mental calculation. With a sudden motion she opened her purse and took out a small notepad with an equally small pencil attached by a loop of yarn. Charlie watched as she wrote on a page, tore it out, and handed it to him.

"Mary Stines," he read aloud. "That you?"

"That's my mother's phone," she said, continuing to give him an unsettling stare. "If you decide you really do want to go dancing."

It was flattering and disturbing in equal measure, this woman being so forward with him. He nodded and made a show of slipping the paper into his pocket. For a moment she seemed to wait for him to say something but he couldn't imagine what. They finished the ride in silence.

As soon as the bus came to a stop at the Asheville station, Mary lurched down the aisle and Charlie considered following her, but by the time he gathered up his jacket and checked his wallet, she was out of sight. It was just as well. He had four dollars and a nickel. He wasn't going dancing with anyone tonight.

■ ■ ■

"Need a ride, sailor?"

Tucking his wallet into his trousers, Charlie looked up to see a cabbie in a BlueBird Taxi. "I'm gonna hoof it, thanks."

"Hop in," the cabbie said. "You going home? You don't want to show up in dusty crackerjacks. This ride's on me."

The cabbie had a point. It would take him the better part of an hour to walk to his grandmother's address, the last stretch of the way on a dirt road. How much better to simply appear as if out of thin air, his starched blue "crackerjacks"—the Navy's cheeky jargon for the enlisted men's blues—neat and crisp, or as neat and crisp as they could be after the eight hours in three different buses on a relay from the port at Charleston.

As soon as he settled into the backseat, the taxi started forward. Charlie met the driver's eyes in the rearview mirror.

"Your wife know you're coming?"

"What?"

"The lady of the house. She know you're back in town?"

"Yeah. She knows."

The cabbie snickered. "Good, good. Always a good idea to let your lady know you're on the way so she can let any *visitors*

make a timely getaway." He laughed again, louder and coarser, pleased with himself.

Charlie gave a half-smile. "I'm going to see my grandmother."

The cabbie draped his right hand over the wheel and shifted in his seat. "Oh, yeah?"

"Gonna collect my nest egg she's holding for me and figure out what to do next."

He felt a vague uneasiness about talking so openly to this stranger, his personal business slipping out before he could stop himself. He'd done this before, being too trusting too fast and then getting pranked or teased or stolen from. Pickpocketed in New York while he stood on the sidewalk gaping at the skyscrapers. Overcharged in a bar in Miami for

*Charlie weighed the wisdom of giving the actual number, which he had calculated to the penny, with the pleasure of boasting a little.*

whisky so watered down that it barely raised his temperature.

The cabbie looked back over his shoulder. "What does that mean—collect your nest egg? What's that?"

"My service money," Charlie said, forgetting his resolve to be more circumspect. "My grandmother's been saving my pay."

The cabbie whistled through his teeth. "Ain't that something! How much we talking about?"

Charlie weighed the wisdom of giving the actual number, which he had calculated to the penny, with the pleasure of boasting a little. "Enough," he said, "to buy a car and start living my life."

"Wow! Such a young guy, too. Coming home rich!"

"Well, not rich. Not yet anyway."

"But a car! You have enough to buy a car. Most guys can't do that."

The road spooled under the wheels of the taxi and Charlie was warmed by the cabbie's praise. Few sailors he knew were going home with money. He could have done what they did, spent his money on decent cigarettes and booze and gifts for some of the girls he met in port instead of squirreling it away. He allowed himself a moment to gloat.

"I guess I'm lucky," he said, attempting—and failing—to sound modest. The cabbie shook his head.

"Oh no, no, no," he said. "Not lucky. Smart. You worked smart and now you have your—what did you call it, nest egg? You have that to show for it."

"Yeah, I—"

"But you know, you might be a lucky guy, too. What do you think?"

"Maybe."

"You know, you ought to take that nest egg and do something with it!" The cabbie banged the flat of his hand on the lip of the steering wheel.

Charlie jumped. "I told you. I'm going to buy a car."

"I know. And that's good. But what about the rest of the money? Before you know it, you're gonna blow it all and then you won't even have enough to pay for gas to run your fancy car. No, you ought to take that money and expand it. Make it grow for you."

"Yeah, but how?"

As soon as he said it, Charlie felt the hair on the back of his neck prickle, the way it had when he'd been on watch when electrical storms skittered over the ocean or his sleep was interrupted by the sudden whine of the klaxon.

The cabbie's eyes were bracketed by the rearview mirror. "I probably shouldn't tell you this, since you don't know me from

Adam's off ox, but there's a poker game meets at Whimbey's every night. Not all high rollers, but some. You could take that cash and double it, triple it, lucky guy like you."

"I don't know."

"Look, like I said, you don't know me. You decide you want in, call me. I'll get you in."

The tips of Charlie's ears were hot, whether from nervousness or excitement, he wasn't sure. "What's in it for you?"

"Nothing but a small finder's fee," the cabbie said. "They don't let just anybody into Wimbey's."

"I'm not that good at poker." Charlie had played plenty of card games on the ship—even for money on the sly when the CO wasn't around.

"You don't have to be good," the cabbie said. "Just lucky, and boy, I can tell that you are one lucky man. Sure, you might be happy with your little nest egg, but you could have the whole fucking golden-egg-laying goose. You know, like in the story."

"I'll think about it." Charlie wasn't afraid of risk. Three years, two months, six days in the Navy made him, if not comfortable, at least willing to face it as stone-cold as anyone else eyeing the wake of an oncoming torpedo. And the cabbie might have a point about making his money grow.

Soon Charlie recognized a series of bungalows on a dirt road, each painted a drab version of green or beige.

"There," Charlie said. "At the end of the street."

"Don't forget what I said." The cabbie handed Charlie a card. "Lady Luck won't wait forever."

■ ■ ■

His duffel bag hoisted over his shoulder, Charlie picked his way around rain puddles like a timid cat. The house, small and the shape and color of a Monopoly piece, seemed to be in good condition—far better than he'd expected. Someone had scraped and repainted the siding, and there were shutters now on the front windows. Most surprising of all—given his own peripatetic childhood—was that his grandmother still lived here.

Before he could knock, the front door swung inward. His grandmother wiped her hands on her apron and leaned forward to hug him. It embarrassed him, this public show of rare affection, and he stepped back and motioned behind him to the muddy yard. "What happened to your grass?"

"You weren't here to take care of it." He heard the hurt in her voice—she'd noticed his stiffness—and for a wild moment he imagined sprinting up the street to flag down the retreating cab.

*Before he could knock, the front door swung inward. His grandmother wiped her hands on her apron and leaned forward to hug him.*

"Well, I'm here now." A peace offering if she'd take it, though she held grudges and could be prickly when annoyed.

"Where's Earl?" his grandmother said, looking past him to the street.

Earl was his grandmother's youngest son who, as far as Charlie knew, still lived with her. Squat and short, he had a quick temper and a ready fist—two things that had prompted Charlie to move to the Y.

"I haven't seen him," Charlie said. His grandmother shook her head.

"He went to the bus station to pick you up. Where'd he go?"

His grandmother's expression was distant, her question rhetorical. Earl was at a bar, or a liquor store, or at the local pawn shop scrounging up enough to go to a bar or a liquor store.

She turned and went into the house, her resignation and weariness as visible to Charlie as if he had never been away. He followed her inside.

A cacophony of voices rushed at him. He struggled to connect them to the faces crowded in the front room: aunts and uncles and cousins, babies he didn't recognize and old people whose familiar features had surrendered to time and gravity since he'd seen them last. They made a happy circle around him and he was touched that they were there, that they'd shown up to welcome him home.

"Give Sonny some air," his grandmother scolded. Laughter, and a shuffling of feet. Charlie jumped, startled at being called by his childhood nickname. *Sonny. Get up, Sonny, we have to be out before the sun is up. Don't take two helpings, Sonny. No, you can't keep that cat, Sonny.* He'd stopped being Sonny the minute—the second—he signed his name on the enlistment papers. Signed them with the unformed loops and whorls of someone who hadn't had enough schooling to know the proper way to write. Signed them like someone leaving one world behind and trying on a new identity.

He felt his duffel lifted from his shoulders and saw it placed reverently on the ground at his feet. A young woman he didn't know pressed her fingers on his forearm and introduced herself as his cousin Ronnie's wife. That couldn't be right, Charlie thought. Ronnie was several years younger than he was—but no, there was Ronnie, a thin-bristled mustache like Rhett Butler's on his lip, a crease pressed into his brow. His uncle Wallace sidled up and put out his hand. Baffled, Charlie shook it, unsure of the reason for such a formal gesture.

One after another the guests made their way to him and spoke. He felt like a movie star or a prince, surprised by the tributes but pleased by them, too. He'd gone away a mere kid and returned a celebrity to a brighter place. The furniture looked less shabby than he remembered. A Crosley radio played music from a wooden end table next to an upholstered sofa.

"Is this rug new?" he said, reaching down to rub the white muzzle of an elderly black dog that wandered up to him.

But his grandmother was gone, the sound of performative banging coming from the kitchen. Charlie let out a breath he seemed to have been holding since he boarded the Greyhound.

"Come take a load off," he heard someone say. His aunt Ida—his grandmother's oldest child—perched at one end of the sofa, patting her hand on the cushion. Unlike her mother, she was rail thin and almost as tall as Charlie. When he still lived with his grandmother, Ida visited often. She read to him while he sat in her lap—newspapers, magazines, Grimm's Fairy Tales. The first shirt he owned that wasn't a hand-me-down or a charity box donation was one she sewed for him from an old tablecloth. Another time Ida handed him a bouquet of wrapped lollipops and told him not to let the other children know. He had no idea why, though he suspected she had witnessed his older cousins inflicting some mischief on him and was, with her adult misunderstanding of the casual cruelty of children, trying to bring justice to bear.

"It's so good to have you home," she said when he settled himself next to her on the sofa. "You've been such a help."

It was an odd turn of phrase, a version of which he'd heard several times since disembarking in Charleston: *Welcome home, sailor. Thank you for your service.*

Charlie blushed. He'd been a ship's cook, not a hero.

"I don't know what Mother would have done without you," Ida said. "Earl hasn't been the biggest help, you know."

"Sure," Charlie said, not at all sure what Ida meant.

Charlie's grandmother appeared in the center of the room. "Time to eat!" she said. "Come make a plate and find a place to sit." People started to rise but Charlie's grandmother shouted again and they froze in place. "A blessing! We have to say a blessing first!"

This was new. Had his grandmother found religion? That's what people said about new zealots, wasn't it? That they'd *found* religion, like an explorer stumbling across an undiscovered continent, or a pirate finding gold in the sand.

He knew what it meant to say a blessing, even if he'd never seen his grandmother do it. Charlie lowered his head and pressed his eyes half shut.

"Oh, Lord," his grandmother began, "we thank you for bringing Sonny home to us from that terrible war. We cried out to you in our distress and you gave him to us, safe and whole. We pray that he continues to help us through these difficult times. Thank you for this meal, in Jesus's name, Amen."

The people around him murmured *Amen*, but Charlie was busy puzzling over the words of his grandmother's prayer. It was out of kilter in some way he couldn't quite place. The words were wrong, or at least not quite right. Or perhaps hearing a prayer in his grandmother's voice was the problem. It was almost as disconcerting as watching those captured German boys praying over their meals. After their wounded U-boat slid beneath the dark gray waves, nine enemy sailors had been hauled up, shivering with cold and fear and taken to the galley for warm coffee and blankets. One with dark brown hair and almost-colorless eyes had asked for sugar—politely, and in English that spoke of an education far better than any of his captors.

But what struck Charlie then—and haunted him still—was how young the nine German sailors were. The nine German *boys*. As a boy himself he saw immediately how sparse their facial hair was, how thin their wrists and fingers were. He saw the acne and the way they blinked their eyes like frightened kittens. More than anything else during his tour of duty, he saw himself in them, and he carried that image home as a sacred memento.

"You coming?" Ronnie's wife stood before him, waving her hand toward the kitchen. Already people were making their way back into the front room, balancing laden plates and glasses of iced tea. "They shoulda put you at the head of the line," Ronnie's wife said, snaking her way through the crowd to the kitchen, Charlie in tow. "Only's fair, since you paid for it."

There it was again, the odd comment, the elevation to self-sacrificing hero that made him squirm. "All those guys who died," Charlie said, "they're the ones who paid. Not me."

*More than anything else during his tour of duty, he saw himself in them, and he carried that image home as a sacred memento.*

Ronnie's wife frowned. "I meant the food. Come get something to eat."

Confused, Charlie took a plate from a stack and surveyed the kitchen table. It was jammed with bowls of crowder peas and corn on the cob and mashed potatoes and green beans and sliced pickled beets and angel biscuits and one tremendous platter of fried chicken. It was more food than he could ever remember seeing at his grandmother's house, more even than Thanksgiving or Christmas or his birthday. It made him uneasy.

In the front room all the chairs were filled by the time Charlie made his way back. Opening the door, he saw Ronnie sitting at the top of the brick steps. Careful not to tip his plate, Charlie eased himself down beside him.

"So," Ronnie said, "what you planning to do now? I mean, now that you're home?"

"Not sure. Might see if the Biltmore will take me back on."

"Really? The hotel? I thought you might be gonna go into the chicken business with Earl."

"Chickens? What's Earl doing with chickens?"

"I musta misunderstood," Ronnie said, spearing a green bean. "I thought you and Earl was gonna raise chickens. They say they's good money in chickens. Thought that's why he's building the pens out back."

"Earl's raising chickens?" He couldn't stop repeating himself. The image of Earl—his shiftless uncle Earl, the one who split Charlie's ear with a drunken punch one afternoon—doing anything productive was astonishing. How could he start a chicken business? Where had he gotten the gumption? Or the money?

*Or the money.*

Charlie stared unseeing across the muddy yard, the food in his mouth turning to ashes. He set the plate down on the steps.

"You okay? Sonny?"

From the end of the road came the stutter of a Ford truck, black and ancient and smoky. It pulled up to the yard and stopped.

"Well, looky who's here!" Earl opened the driver's side door and stepped out heavily. He wore faded denim overalls over a white undershirt, unlaced boots and a brimmed hat. Everything about him was bigger than Charlie recalled—his protruding belly, his hammy arms, his rosebud nose. Charlie started down the steps, uncertain what he would do.

When he was almost sixteen, three weeks into his first posting on a destroyer, Charlie thought he was going to die. He'd been aboard long enough to have gotten used to the constant roll and pitch of the ship, the rocking of his hammock, the communal toilets, the shouts of the cooks and stewards and bakers, the heat of the galley, the weevils in the flour, the sleepy watches, the constant need to paint every part of the ship exposed to the relentless salt of the sea. And then it happened. The first submarine he ever saw materialized off the starboard bow and Charlie and everyone else raced to general quarters. In an instant Charlie understood a phrase he'd heard recently— *sitting duck*. One moment the destroyer was an imposing metal bulwark against danger. The next—a literal sitting duck, waiting for a torpedo to slice through it with a kill shot.

The loss of faith in the ship shook him to his core. It was as if every organ in his body shifted, his stomach emptying, his nervous system jangling so hard that he felt electricity buzzing his fingertips and toes. The sky shifted, too, or his way of seeing it did, and the grays and blacks and blues of the sky and ocean melted and fused into an indeterminate hue.

The torpedo plowed across the distance and Charlie was going to die. He had lied about his age to be here and now he was going to die, a fifteen-year-old faker, a child who had no business anywhere near the war. He was going to die without having done more than kiss a girl and masturbate furtively alone in his bunk. He'd never bought a car and now he never would. He regretted throwing away his youth as his muscles and bones supernaturally aged and braced for his death.

Later, when he *didn't* die, he stretched one hand in front of his face, looking for tremors. The knocking he felt inside did not show: to the outward eye, he was steady and unmoved. Only he knew the truth, that his assurance in the constancy of things was shivered with tiny hard-won cracks. His world tilted on its axis.

Now it shifted again as he slipped and slid across the red clay mud toward his uncle. The recently painted house, the new furniture, the Crosley radio, his uncle's chicken coops, even his own homecoming dinner—he'd bought it all. His fury towered over him and his disappointment was so deep he thought he would drown. There was no nest egg. His grandmother had spent it—out of desperation or greed or stupidity or misunderstanding, it didn't matter. There would be no Lincoln Continental or dancing at the Gloria or courting Eloise. There was nothing at all—not even a lousy job washing dishes or a cot at the Y. His grief was as wide and terrible as winter on the Atlantic, as shattering as learning that those nine German boys were later imprisoned and tortured.

The world tilted, and he with it.

Earl watched him tack his way across the yard. "Don't you look fancy in your Navy duds," he said. Scorn? Jealousy? Charlie heard both in Earl's tone. He held out his hand.

"Hey," he said, his voice muddled and thick, "I need to get cigarettes. Let me borrow your truck. Be right back."

For a moment Charlie thought Earl was going to refuse, but then he shrugged and tossed the keys.

The truck smelled of grease and whiskey. The engine grumbled to life and Charlie eased the gear into first. Where the dirt turned into pavement, he pressed his foot to the gas as hard as he could and felt the satisfaction of the wheels spinning in place before the road shot him forward.

Toward what he didn't know. The recruitment office was closed by now, and the manager at the Biltmore Hotel would have gone home. He considered driving past Eloise's house one last time but turned towards town instead, where he knew there was a dance tonight, and a card game.

If he wanted to, he could drive until the gas ran out, or his four dollars and a nickel were spent. Maybe Lady Luck would let him get all the way to Charleston where he'd take the truck out on the beach and watch the sun come up. There was no hurry. The important thing was to keep moving. The movement was what mattered, the way the ocean and the sun were always in motion. It didn't matter if he was moving *to* something or *away* from something, because they were really the same thing—going and coming, running from the landlord or running to the Navy, arriving home hopeful or leaving heartbroken. Blood traveling through arteries and veins, the seasons melting into each other, stars tumbling across the night sky—he was part of that movement. Wobbly and unsteady, but moving, moving, like someone trying not to get carsick in the mountains, waiting for the chance to glide. ■

# IN PRAISE OF DEAD LEAVES

Our yard's surrounded by trees:
oaks, birches, choke-cherries.
My grandfather called the last
*trash trees*, because they were short-
lived and invasive. Gusts swirl
a fall harvest of leaves that
kaleidoscope on the sinking
grass. The rush reminds me how
my long-dead mother hired
a local boy to wield a rake
and sweep the waist-high pile
of gold and orange and red
into a roadside ditch.
She'd say, *It's always
good to be useful.*

Soon, when my asparagus fronds
die back, I'll cover the bed
with fallen leaves. Mulch deeply
for next season's growth.

**KAREN KILCUP**

# IN PRAISE OF SKUNKS

Put aside your prejudices—
they're lovely, they're plush.
They brim with cuteness.
It's rumored that, de-scented,
they make affectionate pets,
like a cat, but with greater
potential to scare the masked
man who wants to break into
your home and carry off
your computer, jewelry, cash.
Wouldn't the world be better
if we could learn to love all
the creatures that give us pause?
If we could only appreciate
those who mind their business,
leave you alone to yours,
unless they're cornered?

**KAREN KILCUP**

# PINK
# DIAMONDS

AUDREY WICK

T he pickup lunged forward before its diesel engine brought it to a noisy stop. Idling, the cab reverberated in a less than tranquil rhythm, contrasting to the otherwise peaceful and soundless autumn air under a midnight sky.

Rodney rocked in the driver's seat, shifting his weight as he reached his hand into his back jeans pocket, pulling out a billfold as worn as his faded Wranglers. "Pink Diamonds," he announced, proud like a first-time hospital papa. He scissored a $100 bill between his fingers, teasing it toward Kelsie. "Happy birthday, Baby." A sly smile split between his jowly cheeks. "Get ten of them Diamond scratchers."

Lottery tickets were Rodney's vice, not hers. Still, angering Rodney by saying so wasn't a fight Kelsie was willing to have. Not tonight. She accepted the bill, wishing instead he would have bought her an actual gift.

Something guaranteed.

Like much of their relationship, the hope of catching a lucky break seemed like an empty pursuit.

"Thanks," she mouthed before opening her own door and heading into the twenty-four-hour convenience store. Technically, it wasn't even her birthday anymore. He could have done this before their time at the bar that had stretched too long, but Rodney's pipeline job ran late, setting them back—so he said.

At least she had a night out. That was nice. But the fanfare of years gone by was missing. What were birthdays for in adulthood anyhow? Just bitter reminders of unfulfilled milestones and empty years? Kelsie heaved a heavy sigh.

Inside the fluorescent-lit store, counter displays and rows of gawdy impulse purchases screamed for attention. Ignoring them all, Kelsie marched to the rolls of glossy, rectangular tickets held behind a plexiglass case. She pointed to the flashy pink and silver ones, Rodney's favorites. "Pink Diamonds. Ten, please."

The man behind the counter tugged at the roll, soundlessly counting as his head nodded ever so slightly with each ticket that he pulled. Folding them in a hasty Jacob's Ladder, he exchanged them as Kelsie handed over the $100 bill. A cordial "good luck" comment would have buoyed her a bit, but there were no kind words from this stranger.

Men were a perpetual disappointment.

In the silence, Kelsie imagined the tune of the birthday song instead, her own wishes of *happy birthday to me* substituting for an otherwise silent encounter.

The glossy sheen of the crisp tickets reflected the lights as she headed back out the door, though it was hard to see them clearly as the corners of her eyes grew moist. The smallest acts sometimes produced the most feeling, at least for her. Rodney, by contrast, felt things in life differently. She was still trying to understand him.

"Gonna be your lucky night, eh?" Rodney rubbed his palms together as Kelsie hoisted herself into the cab. "Good odds on the Pink Diamonds. Winners here for sure."

"I hope so." Kelsie swallowed her emotions as she leaned in to give Rodney a kiss on the cheek, though contact was more stubble than skin.

"Come on," he urged. "Get to scratching." He let out a low-bellied howl, some cross between drunken excitement and animalism. Rodney was always a bit of a boar.

It was a twenty-minute drive through two FM roads and county backroads to the farm they shared. Kelsie grabbed a penny from the loose change in the ashtray, and holding the first ticket against her knee, she started scratching.

"Scratch the lucky numbers first."

"I know how these work."

"But there's a way."

"Your way?" She cut her gaze to him, but he didn't seem to feel her look.

"The right way."

Rodney's way.

She scratched faster in easy horizontal lines. A string of lucky numbers across the top of each ticket revealed the goal: match one of those numbers to any in the grid below, and win the prize listed for that number. Rodney always scratched the luckies first, and only after parading around with the confirmed winning ticket to whoever was within his sight line would he then scratch to reveal the win. Kelsie preferred a different technique. She wanted to know what she was playing for on the front end—but since it was Rodney's money, she did things his way.

There were a half dozen chances to win on each ticket, but every lucky number felt like someone else's chance. None of the numbers were her favorites: no 13, 23, or 42.

"First one's a bust," she announced.

Rodney spit some curse words. "Keep going, Baby. You're just saving for the big winner."

*Kelsie tried to make her own joy in the moment, telling herself that the experience of hope and anticipation was supposed to be part of the fun.*

The night already felt like a loss. Maybe these expensive pieces of paper were just mirroring that.

Using the rhythm of the country music from the radio, Kelsie tried to make her own joy in the moment, telling herself that the experience of hope and anticipation was supposed to be part of the fun. But it never was for her in the way it was for Rodney. Instead, her emotions felt heavier with every failure.

"Come on. What's that one got?" Rodney's eyes darted from the road to her lap and back again.

"Nothing."

"Loser?"

She chose not to reply to that.

It wasn't until the fifth ticket that there was a break-even win.

"See, odds are looking up." Rodney gave an affirmative nod.

She tore the winning ticket at its perforation, setting the losing ones on the bench seat between them. The silver shavings that were curling from the tickets in the wake of her scratching were peppering her jeans. Kelsie always hated that gritty coating.

Still, she went back to scratching.

After the final ticket, she kept her head bowed. Rodney spat more curse words before asking, "Nine of them are all no counts?"

"Looks to be." Though the tears that had threatened to spill all night were damming at her lids, Kelsie was determined to keep them there.

"Give me 'em." Rodney took the two strips of semi-scratched tickets, rolled down the window, and tossed them into the obsidian night.

Men were as predictable as they were disappointing.

■ ■ ■

With the sun at her back, the cyclist pedaled past the farmland of the gently rolling county roads. Streams of morning light cast entertaining shadows that she chased, one rotation at a time.

Around a curve where the Johnson grass was growing low, a glint caught her eye.

Applying the brakes and then clipping out of the pedals, she eased off the side of her bike to retrieve four discarded lottery tickets, half scratched but still inked. Dipping her head, she tucked them into her waist pouch, next to the used energy gel foil she'd throw away at home. Trash belonged in a receptacle, after all, not on the road. She wouldn't chance these blowing across the fence line near the herd of cattle. The young calves were curious, and this was not something that needed to end up as their cud.

She rolled her thumb and forefinger together, absently grinding to soften the excess silver solvent that her fingerpads had picked up from the top of the tickets. Raising her chin, she was almost ready to start again on the road when another glint stole her attention.

She hoisted herself fully off the bike, walked it forward, and picked up one more set of tickets, folded at the perforations but still intact. Holding them at arm's length like Santa reading a Christmas list, two digits on the top ticket caught her eye. The first lucky number was her own age. Quickly scanning the grid below, she saw it repeated.

That meant one thing: a winner. ∎

# ATAVISIMS

An infant's face is an atlas
of extinct physiognomies.

A great-grandmother's chin.
A father's eyebrow ridge.
An auntie's cheekbones.
A cousin's lips.

An infant's face is a bulwark
of temporal continuums.

Ancestral fever dreams.
The fervid hopes of emigrants.
Assimilationist trauma.
The quixotic aspirations of immigrants.
All-consuming labor.
The blazing success forged of sacrifice.

An infant's face is a palimpsest
of family lore and narrative silence.

The great-grandmother with
a narrow chin and large ears:
ostracized for fleeing
a wartime marriage in exchange
for a woman and a new lease
on what was left
of all too short a life.

The father with
firm eyebrows:

how they cantilevered over
honey brown eyes that melted
the North's wintry disposition and
mid-century women's mores.

The auntie with
the taut cheekbones:
chortling laughter and babbling gossip
that drew in elder and babe at every gathering,
before the cancer darkened
everyone's heart.

The cousin with
the Rubenesque smile:
in self-imposed exile beyond kin and ken,
distancing voice and memory
of a licentious father who wooed and wooed,
neglecting all fealty.

An infant's face is all this and more:
genealogical topographies waiting
for tectonic ruptures and unknown eventides.

**HORACIO SIERRA**

# PAT AND THE SODA MACHINE

A buffalo nickel plunks into the metal ether.
A fizzy soda pops out colder than the ice box.

Pat hands me another nickel, tells me
to be ready for the swift jab and sudden glee.

"Watch and learn."
A Dooly County woman's wizened cue.

She elbows the return slot and jabs two buttons at the same time.

"The soda folks don't know we're getting two for free."
A tarry tincture of one-upmanship.

This was a Depression Era-baby secret,
handed down from clever aunt to awed nephew.

In a town pummeled by heat and regret,
this feat of the mind helped us make due
with what was abuse and what was neglect.

A bounteous harvest not of the cotton that once
made this area rich, but a jugular fountain
of carcinogenic sweeteners that gave us bounce
but not enough fuel to change life's course.

**HORACIO SIERRA**

# POOSEY

EMILY WARREN

**W**e stand before it in silence, like we are consuming the last moments of a dying wild animal. The roof has separated from its sheathing. Vines from the yard braid themselves with the fallen electrical wires no longer in use. Between black shutters, grey sheets of plywood have been nailed over the windows, a project my dad must have started during one of his elusive trips down home. The wooden barriers guard us from whatever it is they conceal on the other side. At the edge of the sunporch, a mulberry tree, leafless and boney, drags its branches along the gutter. The sound of it croaks, like the house is gasping for breath.

It's the day after Christmas. Dad and I have come back here with my sister, Julie, and her family to view the house and the land on which it sits. Before the holiday, my mother sent an email to Julie and me that had reached us in our different cities; Julie in New York and me in Tennessee.

"Sometime when you're both home, we'll need to talk about Poosey." Her subject line read like a warning.

Poosey Ridge is tiny, a stretch of Eastern Kentucky where my father grew up on his parents' tobacco farm. When we were little, he took us there nearly every weekend in the summers to visit his mother, either for Sunday suppers, or just to give our mom a break from being home with us during the week. But two months before I turned six, his mother closed her eyes and died alone in her living room, and we stopped going back. That was almost twenty-one years ago.

In her message Mom described the possibilities she and Dad had talked over. Either the farm could go to us—Julie and me—or the land would be sold, and the profit would be our inheritance. That had always been the intention; that Poosey would be our inheritance, as it had been for our father, and for his father before him, and for the 100 years this place has existed in our family. How that legacy would continue rested with us. It was our decision.

Looking through a broken window at the back of the house, I want to bury what I see: overturned tables and drawers pulled out from an old armoire filled with tattered clothes, empty water jugs, smashed beer cans, broken glass from the light bulbs that still hung over the door on the sunporch. Whoever has done this has used lawn sheers, which now lay lifeless on a pile of trash bags that are mostly still intact. At the top of the door, three consecutive 'K's' are plastered in orange paint.

I remind myself that these are not our things. Years ago, Dad let a woman from the community live in the house when she couldn't afford rent. Their parents had known each other; her father had prepared the taxes for the farm. She had raised her child alone, struggled as a hoarder, and lived off disability checks. When she passed away on Valentine's Day three years ago, her son said he would come clear out what she had left behind. But he never did.

■ ■ ■

Beyond the house on the other side of the road there is a field full of Queen Anne's Lace, and a congregation of headstones that mark graves of people we don't know. They stand in repose under grapevines we imagine are thick enough to hold our weight. The markers are so weathered that the engravings cannot be rubbed into the paper we've brought to record them. Their words, I want to keep. I want to tuck them away to save something tangible, some small bit of proof that we were a breath in the life of this place. I use my fingertips to trace out the edges of names like Abraham, Levi, Lucinda, and Sallie. Some don't have names at all, just the word "infant" and a date carved along its crest, 1794, 1863, 1880. Other stones have been so swallowed by the earth that just the tops peek out like half-moons looming over the blades of uneven grass. When I was little, I would sit with them and wait for Dad and my sister to return from wherever they had gone exploring out on the ridge, usually some steep place I was too small to climb.

It occurs to me that I don't know where his mother is buried. When she died, I wasn't allowed to attend her funeral.

I don't remember the reason they gave me, or why I was the only one in my family not going to her service. On their way to the church, they dropped me off at my uncle's house, where I ate oatmeal and played with my cousins and wondered what it might be like to be sad that she was dead. I couldn't remember the last time I had seen her. I couldn't remember her voice or the way it sounded when she laughed. I didn't know how to miss her or where I could go to hold her hand.

A few weeks after the funeral, my parents left a Bankers Box of her things in our foyer to remind themselves to take to storage on their next trip out. Each time I passed I lifted things from the pile without asking their permission; a tiny metal box lined with pink fabric worn thin at the corners, two sewing stones, a lusterware elephant with a broken trunk, a key.

"She left these for me." I said it out loud, but quiet, so no one could hear me.

■ ■ ■

We collect tobacco sticks from the barn so Julie can have something from the farm to take back with her to the North Country. Her husband wants to use them to build a fence around their home that is perched on the side of a mountain. He was raised under cloud-splitting cliffs of the Adirondacks and follows us in slow motion as if encountering Appalachia for the first time. We move around the barn's perimeter, catching the thin lines of light that break through its contracting planks. The boards separate us from the fullness of the sun and throws shadows onto our clothes and faces.

I imagine there is something inseparable about a person's spirit and the landscapes in which they grew up, even long after they've moved away. I recognize the barn from the scenes Dad would sketch in ballpoint pen across the backs of magazines and into the corners of fast-food napkins. He was a cartoonist and reporter for our local paper, but he's an artist too. His work lines the stairway of our family's house and hangs in churches downtown. It decorates the homes of his friends, and some are in the possession of boyfriends I used to have. Nearly all his work is in some way a reimagining of his memories from Poosey. He spent years recreating the topography through watercolors and oil pastels, with tiny cuttings of balsawood, or scraps of metal he culled from walks around the train tracks behind his office. He gave them to us as gifts, a way for him to process what he still carries. Something unspoken, unadmitted, even to himself.

When I was growing up, he would slip into dreamy tones and talk about some distant relative, or a friend his father had hired out to help with the farm work. He would describe them

*I would hold those stories in the valley of my palm like bits of flint, bang them together to spark my own imagination...*

like legends, like they were old wives' tales featuring characters I was never sure were real or not. I would hold those stories in the valley of my palm like bits of flint, bang them together to spark my own imagination about the people and places he described. I couldn't move or laugh or dance, in case the motion eroded their edges, slipped through my fingers, and left me again.

In my life I have felt the absence of those characters, in the jarring way that an absence can feel like a presence. During tough conversations he had with my mother, I would watch Dad and his tendency to go silent, to disappear into quiet spaces.

"Should we build an addition to the house or not?"

"Can we afford to let the girls go out of state for college or not?"

"Is it better to sell Poosey? Or should we not?"

I would wonder if those characters he told of had been that way too. Was his reluctance to engage a reflection of what they had modeled for him, so that the ability to work through difficult emotions in an honest way, eluded him? I don't think I could have loved him more, but sometimes I wonder, if I had known these parts of his history, could I have loved him better.

When I was young, he drove me to ballet class, and I drew hearts into the dust that gathered on the dash of his pick-up truck. I sat on the countertops of our Saxon house kitchen and asked him to cut apple slices for me before bed. I listened to his voice wind around in his chest as he read to me from the books he thought I might like. During warmer months, I would sit outside and watch him grill vegetables and pork chops for our family. I would sit there in the blue air of summer with my head resting on my fists and watch the ice melt into his gin and tonic, the cold glass collecting sweat in the sunlight. I'd tap the rim and let the droplets cascade down the sides and into a ring on the table.

"Even the glasses are crying," I'd say. He'd hand me a honeysuckle flower, then turn and walk away from me into the early August opus of katydids, oscillating lawn sprinklers, and pork fat burning onto charcoal.

■ ■ ■

On the ridge we go back toward the house and use the cow paths to manage its slopes. The hills move in waves that crash into each other down at the creeks where they meet. We kick at the milkweed seeds with our wellies, the floss rising from the ground and into the air above our heads like moths from an old book.

"It's like visiting a dream," Julie says to me, and doesn't wait for my reply. Instead, she walks past with her husband, their baby strapped to her back. Little Louisa, who is my niece and looks the most like me, who shares my dimples and in six years will stand in front of the tobacco stick fence on her first day of school, ensconced by sunflowers that make her look small. She strains to see me over her mother's shoulder, twisting a curl of amber between her fingers. My eyes touch hers and she smiles at me until she can't look anymore. Like me, she's shy too. So often my older sister and I have moved through the world apart from each other. But in this moment, I wish she would slow down and wait for me, let me catch up, so we can walk it together.

We go back to the car and Julie fastens her daughter into her seat. Our mother is preparing dinner back home in anticipation of the friends we are hosting for the holiday. We have to get back to Lexington. She's waiting for us.

Before he gets to the car, Dad stops again at the base of the house to take it in. I stand beside him, but I don't want him to know I'm there. My sister and I have come back to Poosey unable to speak what both of us already know; that while the farm is intended for us, this place doesn't fit into our lives anymore. And in the aftershock of seeing the house, dilapidated, and dangerous in its state, we know it will have to be torn down. And the land will be sold, and rather than preserving these relics, this piece of us will float away like the milkweed seeds still wafting in the air over the graves and the barn and the crashing green slopes of the ridge.

I stand there with him, knowing that on the other side of all this shattered metal and broken glass is a scene neither of us can stomach. What was left in a vandal's wake are the ruins of someone else's things, but still the shadow of a place we had known.

I see it as it was. I see my grandmother standing at the kitchen sink under a marbled glass window, letting the water from the faucet run over her hands and into the basin below. I see her looking out into the afternoon, the arms of a forsythia bush that used to grow there knocking gently against the panes, reaching, asking politely to be invited inside.

I see my dad as a boy, sitting at the clawfoot table behind her, wearing tennis shoes and eating cornbread with a fork, the sunlight touching the blue eyes I did not inherit. I imagine the way his voice might have sounded, still balanced and soft in his throat, not yet deepened by the vast reflection that comes with loss. I imagine his father walking through a patched screen door carrying a straw hat at his hip, sweat on his face, his hands splintered from hanging tobacco and years of working the land. Silhouetted in the doorway by the leaf-light, he is faceless to me.

I imagine that some grief must escape language, so we carry it around in our bodies where it can go to rest. It pools in the lines on the backs of our hands. It is a fleck of silver in the blackest part of our eye. Our shoulders slope under its weight. I see them standing there in the kitchen and know in my mind I will always go looking for the parts of me that come from them. That what is there, in the room is what has already been lost, and who is still left to be lost. I know that grieving people not fully known to me, is more bearable than facing a day when he's no longer here, standing beside me.

I want to turn to the man gazing at the husk of the home he grew up in, and I want to say it, that it is possible to capture love and grief, painful beauty, and gratitude in a single moment. I want to go up to him in the waning December sunlight and say it.

But the baby is getting sleepy.

My sister's leaving in the morning.

Our mother's waiting for us to come home.

We're expecting company.

So, I say it out loud, but quiet, so he can't hear me. ■

# BACKPACKING

The hike out does it sometimes.
Packing miles through the cold
moss drenched spruce

and the little rivulets of creeks
so near freezing I worry a breath
might send them over that edge,
the water hardening to a clear cement
around the ankles of my boots.

This done, so that I might kneel
in one particular field,

where some long forgotten farmer
has given up tending his corn
or potatoes, and the deer bed down
in the long and warm grass.

Or else, to sit
in some rocky floodplain, where the mountain streams
pour themselves into the cool
& waiting mud

raising a little congregation of cattails
who bow quietly
in the slow, November winds.

I shave down my pencil
with a knife I am always intending to sharpen
and the shavings are blown into the air-
a preface to the first snows

& the story that's there,
I never get it.
But sometimes it makes me happy
to try.

**TANNER HOWARD**

# A PLACE OF OUR OWN

You and me, the little cabin we could have
in the break of a wide river,
a stove pipe brimming from the painted tin
and breathing a long sigh into the cool fog.

There where the river moves slow
and thick as sorghum, ice
bobbing in the water like the heads of salmon
skimming water bugs from the surface.

The doors could be red,
a gentle protest against the canvas
of gray Appalachian mornings,
one apple in a dark, cedar barrel,

a bright, hot heart
pumping rivers of blood
into the freshly fallen snow.

**TANNER HOWARD**

# AT MIDNIGHT

If you squint
Hard enough
Thru the two
Lovers lying
On their couch
In the lamp-lit
Windowpane
You may see
Something move
Out there
In the starless night
Like a shadow
Lurking with
A knife.

**CHASE HARKER**

# HOW THE BODY WRITES

## S. EVAN STUBBLEFIELD

We use it to see the white clapboard house where our character grew up, the old blue Corolla his mother drove him to school in, the Chucks he wore with the torn shoelace and the hole at the toe. We see all of this in our heads as if we had lived it, and so we believe that our imagination is a visual parade in our head. But the profundity in experiencing the imagination is in the body.

We imagine with our senses turned up.

We become the child reaching down to fix our shoe. We feel our hunching forward. We smell the rubbery-mildew of the car floor at our feet. We sense the dashboard at the crown of our head, and feel-see our fingers tying the lace that reaches just halfway up our sneaker. After we're done, the sensation on our right foot is that the shoe, as always, is about to come off, and that sensation of the faulty shoelace reminds us of things we would rather not think about.

*That* is imagination, an experience translated through the body!s memory.

In his book *The Spell of the Sensuous,* phenomenologist David Abram says this about imagination:

> From the magician's, or the phenomenologist's, perspective, that which we call the imagination is from the first an attribute of the senses themselves; imagination is not a separate mental faculty (as we so often assume) but is rather the way the senses themselves have of throwing themselves beyond what is immediately given, in order to make tentative contact with the other sides of things that we do not sense directly, with the hidden or invisible aspects of the sensible.[1]

Thus, without our sense of touch, of smell, of sight, of sound, of taste, without our gut reaction, there is nothing to imagine. The mind dreams and therefore seems to transcend the body, but it's the body that carries the felt experience of transcendence. It's the body that connects to and reacts to

1    David Abram, *The Spell of the Sensuous: Perception and Language in a More-Than-Human World.* (New York: Vintage Books, 1996), 58.

what we experience in our imagination and our dreams. When we're writing with all of our might and our hearts beat with fear or shame or pleasure, as if we were experiencing that very thing ourselves, it!s our bodies that respond.

■ ■ ■

Part of why we disparage the body as a place of wisdom is social, political, and historical. It is analogous to how we!ve been taught to separate people based on race, class, gender, sexuality, religion, and disability. Some people, we are taught, are naturally ignorant, aggressive, unclean, primitive, animal. That's also how many of us regard the natural world, as a place we think of as separate from ourselves. To broadly paraphrase Abram, we see the natural world as a fascinating, but potentially dangerous place. We keep it at arm's length, although, ironically, it!s beside us always, in the environment we pass through and in the bodies we inhabit.

I say this not to get wrapped up in something unrelated to writing and creativity, but to show how completely we've learned to separate mind from body. As creative writers this separation puts us in a conundrum. We wrestle with the societal preference of mind over body while, as E.V. De Cleyre suggests in "Writing the Body," we try to (re-)inhabit our old or other selves by writing poetry, fiction and creative nonfiction. We try to (re-)inhabit those selves because the body allows us into the kind of truth the mind cannot get a fix on, for the body cannot lie.[2]

Good writers write from the body; we listen for what characters want to say; we wait for what is real and true. Good writers default to the mind when the thread of creativity is lost or we face some emotional obstacle that stalls the work. We wait, patiently listening but sometimes fighting against what we hear. We resist ourselves. We force things to be true.

Instead, we could listen to our emotional obstacles. We could explore them instead of avoiding or resisting.

Think of listening to emotional obstacles metaphorically, like walking into a pitch black room and shutting the door. The only thing leading us is our intention. We sit in the dark waiting for some indication of what to write next. Something will show up, but it may require assiduous attention, deep listening, commitment to the process. Whatever arises, obstacle or doorway, we acknowledge because there are story roots there. If nothing arises, we wait. Something will show up. When it does, we write it down as best we can. Write and wait, write and wait until the process is complete.

Some of what we get will be relevant to story, some of it will be personal. Record all of it. Instead of looking for a way to avoid the obstacle, we must use it to look for the light. It's like going toward what scares us. At first we're terrified, certain we're going to die, but we don't. Afterwards everything is easier.

It's in fear that the gift lies.

Listening to the body requires a patience both deep and long. Patience met with a great deal of latitude when we don't get the answers we anticipated or when we get no answers at all. Patience is something writers have quite a lot of. No one impatiently writes a 300-page novel, a book of poems, a memoir, a prize-winning short story. This practice of listening to the body, of inspiring truth into the chaos of our lives, would then seem worth the wait. ■

---

2   E.V. De Cleyre, "Writing the Body: Ta-Nehisi Coates, Maggie Nelson & Lidia Yuknavitch." Blog.pshares.org. Network Solutions, LLC, 17 Aug. 2015. Web. 21 May 2015.

# CELEBRATION OF LIGHTS

Kent, Connecticut 2021

We stopped believing
as kids but who can't
appreciate eggnog
lattes, or a flush
of rainbow lights
after a short gray
glum day? Weeks
ago we met a friend
also thirty something
also a longtime skeptic
of *family* and *home*
at a fire department
holiday parade. All
three of us balancing
our array of traumas,
hot cocoa cup in one
glove, smartphone in
the other. We snapped
photos as Santa, elves,
grinches on glowing
truck beds, trailers,
and wobbly bicycles
waved and sang to
crowds masked and
unmasked. The entire
event—*past*—within
minutes. We froze
next to our cars after,
searched for satellites.

All anchored to cold
by clear sky, our need
to shiver and share
without trying to make
sense of what doesn't.

**ALISON TERJEK**

# COPING, OUTSIDE THE LINES

You interrupted this poem
with a hug, asked *will this
make it better or worse?*
My answer—that depends.
You're a part of it now.
If you caught me in a night
terror would you shake my
shoulder? Keep me company?
Do you know any jokes that
don't end with me falling flat?
I've built a shrine to heavy
blankets, adult coloring books,
sharpened pencils. You're
free to join. I've coaxed
black and white flowers to life.
I know the general location
of my door knob but not how
to turn. What color would you
make this butterfly? Do you
think it'll fly if we sketch it
a way out? Should we try?

**ALISON TERJEK**

# AFTER
# JIMMY

**COURTNEY HILL GULBRO**

I heard the motorcycles in the driveway just before bedtime. Jimmy had never shown up so late or unannounced, and I ran outside to see him. In the yard, Jimmy's friend Sonny stayed back a ways as Jimmy took off his helmet and headed toward the porch. I could smell beer and detected a wobble in his stride. I knew he drank some, but he never had around me.

"Hey," he said. I said *hey* back. It was odd that he didn't walk right up to me like usual. I smoothed my skirt, still dressed from work at my dad's jewelry store. Lightning bugs flickered as the Alabama heat eased, and soft sounds from my parents' conversation floated through the window screens.

"What are y'all doing up here?"

"Just out riding around."

Jimmy shifted from one foot to the other and then said, "I think we need to break up."

I'm pretty sure I stopped breathing. I looked over at Sonny who was studying his handlebar. The leaves fluttered, backlit by the post light on the sweetgum tree, their shadows chasing each other across the yard.

I stood on the bottom step of the porch, my lip trembling. "But why?"

Jimmy took a deep breath and tilted his head. "Well, we're going to different schools in the fall."

My mountaintop neighborhood had been rezoned, but I wasn't moving away. My body stung with shock.

Jimmy was my first real boyfriend. My parents didn't approve of our relationship, but they thought it would run its course if they didn't make a big deal about it.

With his sandy brown hair and blue eyes that looked deep into mine, I couldn't resist Jimmy. His navy blue windbreaker always held a whiff of cigarettes. We weren't old enough to drive yet, but he rode a motorcycle everywhere he went. To me he was the epitome of coolness. Every once in a while, Jimmy straddled the line of the law. One time he and Sonny stole a speaker from the ballfield. It nicked Jimmy's forehead when it fell to the ground and left him with a one-inch scar in the shape of a C. He said this marked him with my initial, and that was surely a sign we were meant to be together. We met at the movies a few times—matinees downtown at the theater near my family's jewelry store. Those kisses in the dark seemed so romantic. On nights Jimmy didn't come to the mountain, we talked on the phone until Mama poked her head in the door and said it was time to hang up and go to sleep. Despite his "bad boy" ways, Jimmy was sweet to me. I had thought we would be together forever.

I don't remember what happened after Jimmy said we were breaking up, but he and Sonny rode off and I went back in the house and threw myself on my bed, crying. Mama settled on the edge next to me, rubbing my back and smoothing my hair from my face. "I know it hurts, sweetheart," she said when she could get a word in. "He does have a point. You're going to different schools now."

I thought of all those afternoons in the spring of ninth grade, Jimmy riding up the mountain to see me, holding hands on the sofa, catching up on what we'd missed since we last spoke after sixth period. I cried harder with a new wave of tears. Mama sat beside me for a while until I calmed and the house quieted. "Things can look better in the morning," she said, and kissed me goodnight.

I stayed awake all night, and somewhere in the middle of darkness I decided I'd go see Jimmy in the morning and talk it out when he was sober. I knew I could get him to see reason. It was going to be a long walk down the mountain, and since my parents wouldn't let me go, I needed to leave well before dawn to get back before they woke up.

I stuffed my teal Bulova transistor radio under my pillow and turned it on real low to make sure I stayed awake. Around four I looked at the bed across from mine to see if my sister Ann was asleep. Her steady breathing assured me she was. Streetlight tinged the white Priscilla curtains fluttering in the breeze, the July air warm and jasmine sweet. The rest of the house was still except for the ticking clock on the living room mantel and Daddy's soft snoring down the hall. I figured I could get out without anyone knowing.

Before the first hint of daylight, I pulled on a pair of shorts and threw a shirt over my nightgown. In the bathroom I splashed water on my face and brushed my teeth, but there was no time for makeup. I didn't like the way my tennis shoes looked on, so I slipped into some comfortable sandals and stepped into the hall, listening to see if anyone was awake, then tiptoed to the front door. I moved quickly across the lawn and up to the street, afraid someone would see me and make me go back. I'd never been out this early or hiked this far, and I'd never gone anywhere off the mountain by myself.

All was quiet as I walked across the top of Monte Sano by the main road. Up the street, my grandmother's place was still dark, as were most of the familiar houses on my route. I developed

*Sometimes when we came home this way, cars parked at the overlooks above the glittering city held lovers or others doing things they didn't want people to see.*

a rhythm to my steps that created a calm determination underneath the bejeweled starlight in the night sky. Every once in a while, the scent of honeysuckle drifted through the air, but the birds and crickets were still sleeping. It would be hours before the stifling summer heat settled in for the day.

Two miles were behind me at the edge of the mountain's 1,600-foot elevation. I rounded the hairpin curves then trekked another three miles down the back side, a winding woods-lined road seldom traveled at night. Sometimes when we came home this way, cars parked at the overlooks above the glittering city held lovers or others doing things they didn't want people to see. But mostly the road was long and dark and quiet. I had plenty of time to think about what had happened the night before.

As my sandals tapped the pavement, scenes forced their way into my mind. Me, handing back Jimmy's ID bracelet in the front yard. There wasn't any good reason for Jimmy to break up with me, and if he hadn't been drinking, he wouldn't have. Or had he been drinking for courage? Was he interested in someone else? He still said he loved me. He'd told me once about a girl who lived near the mall, but he'd called her a whore, and I knew she wasn't like me. No, there was no one else.

Car lights turned the leaves from dark to green; at the curve ahead, the pavement surfaced into view. I darted toward the woods. The car went on by.

*I can fix this*, I reminded myself as I stepped back onto the road. Determination fortified my body. Further down I heard the first flute of birdsong and noticed the pinkish grey of dawn bloom through the trees. I thought for a minute about what would happen if I didn't get home before my parents woke up. Mama's illness the year before never left the back of my mind. She'd been hospitalized for three weeks with a constriction in her brain, placing her at risk of a stroke. The doctor had told us not to upset her. *I can't let her worry about me*, I thought. *I've got to hurry.*

A doe and her young fawn, sensing me nearby, stopped in their tracks. When I got closer, they leaped back into the brush. Daybreak shed light on my surroundings, and I kept walking, getting more concerned I'd be seen and wouldn't get to talk to Jimmy. This was taking longer than I'd realized.

Near the bottom of the mountain I turned at the street that led to Jimmy's neighborhood. The first part of this road was so steep everyone called it Suicide Hill. I walked gingerly down that section, and was relieved when I got through it, but once I was on flat road I fell and scraped my right knee pretty bad. I dusted myself off as best I could, noticing the strap to my right sandal was torn. I kept walking to Jimmy's house, sandal flapping, a ruby trail of blood seeping down my leg.

His dad opened the door, wearing pajamas and a robe. Mr. R. ran a nightclub in town and probably hadn't been home long. "This is mighty early," he said, then called back to Jimmy's mom that it was me. I realized my early-morning knock on the door might have startled them. "Jimmy spent the night over at David's," he said. "I reckon he's still there."

By the time I got to David's house everyone was up. Jimmy and David met me at the door. They glanced at each other, and it was clear from their expressions that neither could believe I was standing in front of them. Jimmy's blue eyes held mine, like always. I was hoping for a little time alone with him to talk.

Instead he said, "I've got to call your parents."

I started to protest—I'd just gotten there, after all—but he was dialing our number. While it always felt good to hear Daddy say how smart and sweet my sisters and I were, with it came the expectation we'd live up to that. I had found myself on the receiving end of some stern talks over the years, and what he said went. I preferred it when he called me his "middlest angel," so I tried to keep my questionable deeds hidden. This might not be one of those times.

"Mr. Hill, do you know where Courtney is?" I stood next to Jimmy in the downstairs rec room at David's.

"I think she went looking for you." I could hear Daddy through the phone Jimmy held to his ear. I ran my fingers through my uncombed mess of blonde hair.

"Yes sir. She's here. We're over at David's house. Do you want to talk to her?"

I took a deep breath as Jimmy handed me the phone.

"Are you okay?" There was concern in Daddy's voice.

I assured him I was.

"I'm on my way. Will you stay right there until I can get there?"

Oblivious to how much I'd frightened them, I wondered why he thought I might leave.

The smell of bacon and biscuits drifted into the room and David's mother came down to see if I wanted some breakfast. "No ma'am. Thank you though. Daddy's on his way to get me." She and David went back upstairs, leaving us alone. Jimmy took my hand, and we sat on the plaid sofa. Those familiar fingers linked through mine were meant to comfort me, but I was starting to feel more than a little embarrassed. Maybe I hadn't thought this through enough before setting out.

"Are you sure you want to break up?" I asked him.

"I really think it's for the best," he said, and shifted to look at my face. "You'll be at Huntsville High and I'll be at Lee. You'll be meeting a lot of new people."

It sounded wise, but still.

I saw the white Ford Galaxy 500 drive up and my father walk to the door, his eyebrows bunched together and his mouth set in a grim line. He was dressed in a suit and tie, ready for the store. Without much discussion I got in the front seat, the red vinyl already sticky from the heat. "Did you get hurt?" he asked, glancing at my knee.

I tried to sound normal. "I'm fine," I said, but wondered how much trouble I was in.

"Your mother and I were *awfully* worried about you." Daddy had a way of emphasizing words. "Something *terrible* could have happened to you walking down this road in the middle of the night *by yourself.*"

I had been so afraid I wouldn't get to talk to Jimmy that I never thought about being in danger, a fifteen-year-old girl alone in the dark for miles on this isolated road.

Daddy left me to my thoughts and it was a quiet drive home. I was surprised but thankful not to be getting more of a lecture. Neither of my sisters— even Nora in her rebellious moments—had ever gone out without permission, especially in the middle of the night. Surely they understood I just meant to talk to Jimmy. I wasn't mad or leaving home or anything. As we drove back up the mountain under the canopy of summer leaves, I hoped everyone would just treat this like nothing to get too excited about.

When we got home Daddy hugged me then kissed Mama and left for work. The look on Mama's face said they'd agreed she'd get to the bottom of things. I could tell she was mad. That in itself was a big deal—I rarely saw my angelic mother angry, and even more rarely had I seen her angry at *me*.

I ran a bath, got in the tub and the door opened. Since becoming teenagers Mama hadn't walked in on us. The water splashed as I covered my body with my arms and looked up

*Daddy left me to my thoughts and it was a quiet drive home. I was surprised but thankful to not be getting more of a lecture.*

at her, her blue eyes dark. "I can't believe you went out by yourself in the middle of the night," she said. I didn't know what to say, so we just looked at each other a minute. "You're going to have to come to the store with me this morning."

I did *not* want to spend all day downtown while she worked in the office. I needed a nap and some time to think. But I wasn't one to argue with her.

While I was getting ready in our room Ann watched from her bed. Finally she spoke. "I was so worried," she said. "I looked *everywhere*. I even opened the door to the refrigerator for some reason, as though you might have left a clue." It sounded ridiculous and sweet at the same time. We both giggled a little. We'd giggled a lot over the years, sharing a room and secrets and worries.

"You could at least have left me a note on that bulletin board," she said.

I looked over at the pink burlap-wrapped board with the daisy Ann had given me for my birthday just two months earlier. I hadn't meant to get everyone so worried.

When we got to the store I glanced in the mirror that rested on the pendant showcase, hoping the events of the night didn't show. Grief and exhaustion were all over my face, my eyes still a little puffy. On the sales floor my grandmother waited on a customer. I glanced at Mrs. J who was checking in a giftware shipment. Her grandchildren were fairly perfect, by her account, and I wondered if she knew what I'd done. She smiled and said "good morning" like usual.

In the office Mama thumbed through the stack of sales receipts from the day before and took the cover off the brown bookkeeping machine. "You girls can go downstairs and put away stock if you want," she said, her eyes gentle now. "There should be some Cokes in the refrigerator." I was grateful for a quiet chore to pass the time.

Daddy was at the workbench in the basement. Over his dress shirt he wore a blue-and-white-striped canvas apron covered in remnants of jewelers' polishing compound and the various chemicals that went into soldering or cleaning or evaluating jewelry. He had the jewelers' loupe over his eye, and with a pair of long tweezers he checked the prongs on a diamond ring he'd just set. Daddy heard our footsteps and looked up at us through the loupe, smiling. "Hi girls," he said. "I'm almost through here then I'll move that box so you can reach it."

He acted like things were normal, so I relaxed just a little. Daddy placed the ring in a small basket and dropped it into the cleaning fluid. The familiar hum of the machine started, and he moved the tall box of china so Ann and I could check in the pieces and shelve them. Then he took off the apron, slipped his suit coat over his dress shirt that was still crisp and white, and headed back upstairs. "Hey darlin'," he said when he reached the top, and I heard my parents kiss. Romantic love permeated my surroundings, and at fifteen I had already lost.

The next night we went up the street to my grandmother's house for supper, which was unusual on a weeknight. She had prepared a feast of roast beef that fell in piles on the platter. Being the middle of July, I'm pretty sure she served her usual fare for that time of year. Next to the window overlooking the patio and backyard the harvest table was set. There were fresh summer vegetables like corn on the cob, steamed yellow squash, deep red Alabama tomatoes sliced thick, and snap beans cooked until they were flat and the seeds slid out the sides. I'm positive she had remembered my favorite Pillsbury biscuits popped from the can, hot with melting butter and blackberry preserves. Before we sat down to eat, she cleared her throat like she wanted to make an announcement. My sweet little grandmother didn't usually make statements before we ate. Daddy typically said the prayer. Sometimes Granddaddy had when he was still alive, but she was on her own now. We stood expectantly in a ring and she said, "This is a Thanksgiving dinner."

*What*? I thought. This is the middle of the summer. Is she getting forgetful?

"We're thankful we have our little Courtney back."

I adored my grandmother, but I really wanted to slide under the rug.

Little else was said of my escapade after that, but my parents kept track of me a little more closely. Grief came in waves, and each time I looked in my closet for something to wear I would think of the last time I wore it when Jimmy and I were still together. He called me later that week to see how I was doing. He had wondered about my sanity when he saw me that morning at David's. That felt kind of weird to hear. It had all seemed so logical to me—I had just wanted to straighten things out.

It wasn't just Jimmy that I was losing. Rezoning my neighborhood took me away from most of my school friends. I didn't think I could stand losing my boyfriend too. Jimmy was my tether to the three years of junior high and all that encompassed. Three years of mornings with my girlfriends, reliving in precise detail the events of the day before. Three years of school, off the isolated mountain during the early years of integration. Going through the assassinations of Martin Luther King Jr. and Bobby Kennedy in a milieu where we talked about these things. Witnessing my mother's illness and fragile recovery. Three years of changes to my mind and body—so different now than that of the twelve-year-old who started seventh grade. Who was I going to be now?

Jimmy called a few more times over the summer, but the relationship dwindled away after that. Summer band started at our new school, and Ann and I had songs to learn and classmates to meet.

A week or two later, my family vacationed at the lake. I went out with a boy whose family was staying in a cabin nearby. His dark blond hair brushed his eyebrows, his eleventh-grade body so different than the junior high kids. We rode in his boat to a dockside restaurant—the first time I'd traveled across water to dinner. My knees knocked against the dashboard as we bumped over the waves and in reflex I reached for the tender place from my fall. I looked down and saw the scab was gone, revealing pearly new skin underneath. ■

# BOOK REVIEW

---

**Alisa Alering.** *Smothermoss.* **Portland, Or.: Tin House, 2024. 256 pages. Hardcover. $17.95.**

*Reviewed by Lindsey Pharr*

Sheila drags an invisible rope behind her: a noose no one can see around her neck. She constricts and restricts herself in constant awareness of her family's poverty, her duties as eldest daughter, and the lengths to which she must go to protect her secrets.

Angie, of course, is Sheila's opposite. She is ball of kinetic energy like a long-limbed puppy covered in mud, immersed in her own fantasy world inspired by *Rambo* movies and zombie apocalypses. But Angie too has her secrets—whispered to her by unseen forces and surfacing in her drawings. She channels these images in a trance-like state and creates a set of tarot-like cards that guide her every move…and the lives of those around her.

When two young women are murdered while hiking the nearby Appalachian Trail, the two sisters become entangled in the ongoing search for the killer roaming their woods. Soon all of their secrets will be brought to the surface. The climax is slow, tension-filled, and orchestrated by forces much older than the human inhabitants of this small mountain community.

The sisters' outsider status stems from the family's poverty, but these protagonists have other traits that set them on the fringes: Sheila struggles with her closeted queerness and disordered eating while Angie is autistic and practically feral. These very real aspects lend gravity to the fantastical elements of the novel and make the sisters come fully alive on the page.

I devoured *Smothermoss* over a couple of days, staying up late into the night and underlining line after line of gorgeous writing. Alering's prose is at turns lyrical and shocking, languid and crackling with suspense. This debut novel is undeniably strange, a literary dark fantasy set in 1980s Appalachia and in a similar vein to Karen Russell's swampy magic and Leigh Bardugo's dark academia horror. There's more than a touch of the Lovecraftian too, an eldritch reek that reminds me of the fiction podcast *Old Gods of Appalachia*. The author's careful attention to the flora and fauna of the region deeply roots the novel in place, seeding the pages with bloodroot and skunk cabbage, foxes and an abundant rabbit motif. In folklore around the globe, rabbits are associated with a wide symbolic range, from fertility to innocence to downright evil. Alering weaves in all of these and the illustrations accompanying each title's chapter enhance the mythological aspect of the novel.

A lush, haunting, and compelling read, *Smothermoss* is the perfect novel to relax with on the banks of a cool stream this summer. Just keep an eye on the deep, dark shadows that are beginning to stretch and awaken just beyond the fern beds. ■

# BACK FROM THE FUNERAL

Daddy's dead but the wash is still wet,
so Mama and I stand side by side
at the strand of fence wire strung between the pecan trees
in the orchard late this breezy afternoon,
her mouth full of clothespins
so no word between us, no sound at all
but our breathing in, breathing out,
as I hand her my cloroxed T-shirts to hang on the line,
the wind filling their sleeves as if with shoulders,
our own shoulders touching,
our own arms splayed like the limbs of these trees
that have sheltered us all our lives,
holding off the setting sun.

**KEVIN NANCE**

# A VISITATION

1
I wake to the scent
of grandma's lilac hand cream
wafting in the air.

2
Do the dead return?
If not, whose fingers are these
pulling at my sleeve?

3
The aroma shifts
to lard, buttermilk, her hands
moving in the flour.

4
Hot from the oven,
her biscuits are ridged on top
where she pressed them down.

5
Her apron comes loose
at the back and she lets me
tie the strings again.

6
I go to bed with
Beechnut snuff and Doublemint
gum, sweet on her breath.

**KEVIN NANCE**

# CONTRIBUTORS

**Skylar Bensheimer** is a graduate of Berea College, where he majored in English and served as a student editor at *Appalachian Review*. He lives in Lexington, Kentucky.

As a book coach and writing teacher for women in Los Angeles, **Jennifer Dickinson** relishes creating safe spaces for women to feel empowered by embracing their vulnerabilities through writing. A graduate of Hollins University in Virginia, her fiction has appeared in *The Florida Review, JMWW, Beloit Fiction Journal, Isele Magazine, Blackbird* and elsewhere. Her nonfiction has appeared in *The Linden Review* and *Poets & Writers* magazine. She is the recipient of a Hedgebrook residency and a grant from the Barbara Deming Memorial Fund. Her middle grade debut novel will be published in 2026. Connect with her at jenniferdickinsonwrites.com

**Adam Edelman**'s work has appeared in *Narrative Magazine, Fugue, Forklift, Ohio, decomP, Bridge, DeLuge, Barnhouse* and *The Raw Art Review*. His chapbook *It's Becoming A Lot More Difficult to Feel Unchanged* won the 2020 UnCollected Press Chapbook Prize. He holds an MFA in poetry from the New Writers Project at the University of Texas at Austin, where he received a fellowship from the Michener Center for Writers, and a PhD in creative writing from the University of Illinois at Chicago. He teaches at Berea College.

**Courtney Hill Gulbro** has returned to writing after a career as a counselor and professor of counseling. She has lived and worked around the world, and now lives in her hometown of Huntsville, Alabama. She is a 2022 graduate of Spalding University's Naslund-Mann Graduate School of Writing with a Master of Arts in Writing. Her work has appeared in *Ponder Review, River Teeth's* "Beautiful Things" and elsewhere.

**Chase Harker** is a native of New Bern, North Carolina. He is a student in the MFA program at UNC-Wilmington. His work has previously appeared in *Flying South, BarBar, In Parentheses* and elsewhere

**Silas House** is the nationally bestselling author of seven novels, most recently *Lark Ascending*, as well as three plays and one book of creative nonfiction. He is a frequent contributor to the *New York Times* and serves as the NEH Chair of Appalachian Studies at Berea College and on the fiction faculty at Spalding University's Naslund-Mann Graduate School of Writing.

**Tanner Howard** is a writer whose work has appeared in several literary journals including *Evocations* and *West Trade Review*. He is a Georgia College and State University alumus from southern Appalachia.

A New Englander with long farming roots, **Karen Kilcup** is the Elizabeth Rosenthal Excellence Professor of American Literature, Environmental & Sustainability Studies, and Women's, Gender, & Sexuality Studies at UNC-Greensboro. Her poetry collection *The Art of Restoration* was awarded the 2021 Winter Goose Poetry Prize, and her chapbook *Red Appetite* received the 2022 Helen Kay Chapbook Poetry Prize.

**John P. Lackey** of Lexington, Kentucky is a painter, printmaker, and writer. Through his art he has worked with Wilco (the band), Larkspur Press, LexArts, Kentucky Arts Council, Kentucky State Parks, Holler Poets Series, University Press of Kentucky, Kentucky Chamber of Commerce, Garden Gate Records, North of Center Newspaper, many of Kentucky's wonderful authors, Fillmore Auditorium Denver, Terrapin Hill Farm and a variety of restaurants. He is a juried member of the Kentucky Guild of Artists and Craftsmen and Kentucky Crafted.

**Kay McSpadden**'s fiction has appeared in *Kestrel, Cobalt* and *Chautauqua*. In 2012 she won the Norman Mailer Center Fiction Prize, and in 2017 she was a finalist in the Tennessee Williams/New Orleans Festival Fiction Contest. A collection of her *Charlotte Observer* op-eds is published as *Notes from a Classroom: Reflections on Teaching*.

**Kevin Nance** is a writer and photographer in Lexington, Kentucky. His two collections of haiku and photographs are *Even If* (University of Kentucky Arts in HealthCare, 2020) and *Midnight* (Act of Power Press, 2022). His poems have appeared in *The North American Review, Willawaw Journal, Screen Porch Review, Poet Lore, Pegasus,*

*Cumberland Poetry Review* and other magazines. His arts journalism has appeared in T*he Washington Post, The Wall Street Journal, USA Today, The Chicago Tribune, Poets & Writers* magazine and other publications. Kevin is the host of *Out & About* in Kentucky, an LGBTQ talk show, and a co-host of *Kentucky Writers Roundtable*, both on RadioLex 93.9 FM.

**Lindsey Pharr** lives and writes outside of Asheville, North Carolina. Her work has appeared in *River Teeth, SmokeLong Quarterly, Assay, Appalachian Review, Longleaf Review, River Teeth*'s "Beautiful Things", and elsewhere. She received her MFA in Creative Nonfiction from the Naslund-Mann Graduate School of Writing at Spalding University. A full list of publications and honors is on her website www.lindsey-pharr.com, and you can find her on Twitter and Instagram @ lindsey_a_pharr.

**Horacio Sierra** is inspired by the way geography, history and culture shape our identities in a pluralistic society. His creative work has been published in *The William & Mary Review, Saw Palm, Gulf Stream Magazine, Peregrine* and *O, Miami*. His journalism has been published in *The Washington Post, The Baltimore Sun, Forbes* and *The Miami Herald*. In 2023, President Biden appointed him to the President's Committee on the Arts and the Humanities. Horacio splits his time between Florida and D.C.

**S. Evan Stubblefield** blames her love of story on threads of unfinished family gossip. She writes to uncover the inexpressible connection between history, ancestors and the deep roots of African-American culture. Her work has appeared in publications including *Good River Review, past-ten, WomenArts Quarterly* and *Minerva Rising*.

**Alison Terjek** is a writer and mental health advocate living in Northwestern Connecticut. She spends her weekends outdoors where she searches for peace and inspiration in the mountains. Her poetry has appeared previously in *Watershed Review, The Healing Muse, RiverSedge, Peregrine, Appalachian Review* and elsewhere.

**Emily Warren** is a writer from Lexington. She is a current MFA candidate at the University of Kentucky. "Poosey" is her first publication.

**Audrey Wick** is a writer and professor of English at Blinn College (Texas). She has authored educational content for Cengage, served on faculty of the San Miguel Literary Sala (Mexico), and been a repeat contributor to *Writer's Digest, Woman's World* and *Chicken Soup for the Soul*, with stories also appearing in various literary journals. Connect with her at audreywick.com, and on X and Instagram @WickWrites.

**Marianne Worthington** is author of *The Girl Singer* (University Press of Kentucky, 2021), winner of the 2022 Weatherford Award for Poetry. Her work has appeared in *Oxford American, CALYX, Chapter 16* and *Cheap Pop*, among other places. She cofounded and served as poetry editor of *Still: The Journal*, an online literary magazine publishing writers, artists, and musicians with ties to Appalachia since 2009. She coedited *Piano in a Sycamore: Writing Lessons from the Appalachian Writers' Workshop* and is author of a poetry chapbook. She grew up in Knoxville, Tennessee, and lives, writes and teaches in southeastern Kentucky.

www.ingramcontent.com/pod-product-compliance
Lightning Source LLC
Chambersburg PA
CBHW070559180626
46817CB00005B/1904